THIS BOOK BELONGS TO

_____

_____

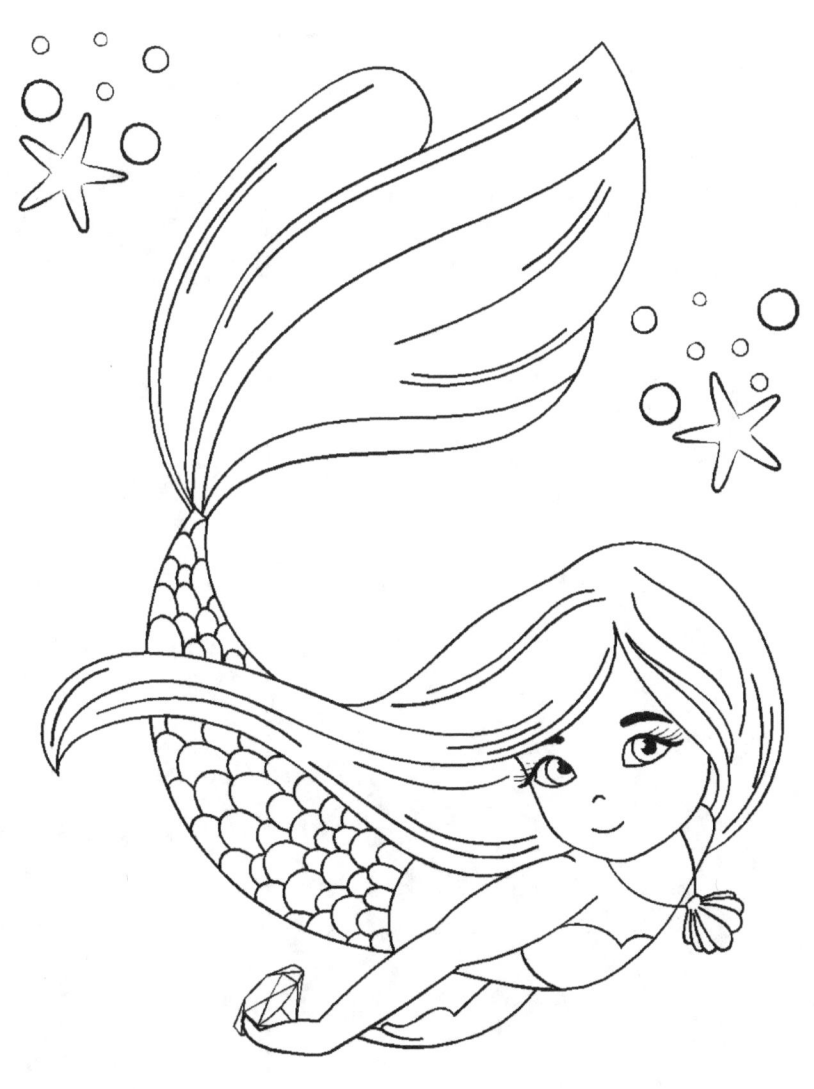

_____

Thank yOu for your purchase!

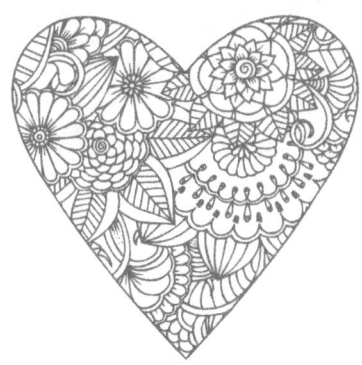

We hope that you are enjoying your new coloring book.
If you would like to leave a positive review on Amazon
we would appreciate your help!

Go to your Amazon account
Click on RETURNS & ORDERS
Search for this purchase and click
Click on "WRITE A PRODUCT REVIEW"

WE HAVE A SPECIAL GIFT FOR YOU!
SCAN THIS QR CODE FOR FREE COLORING BOOK!

VISIT US AT www.lindarheaart.com and check out our BLOG
for more information on coloring tips and tricks!

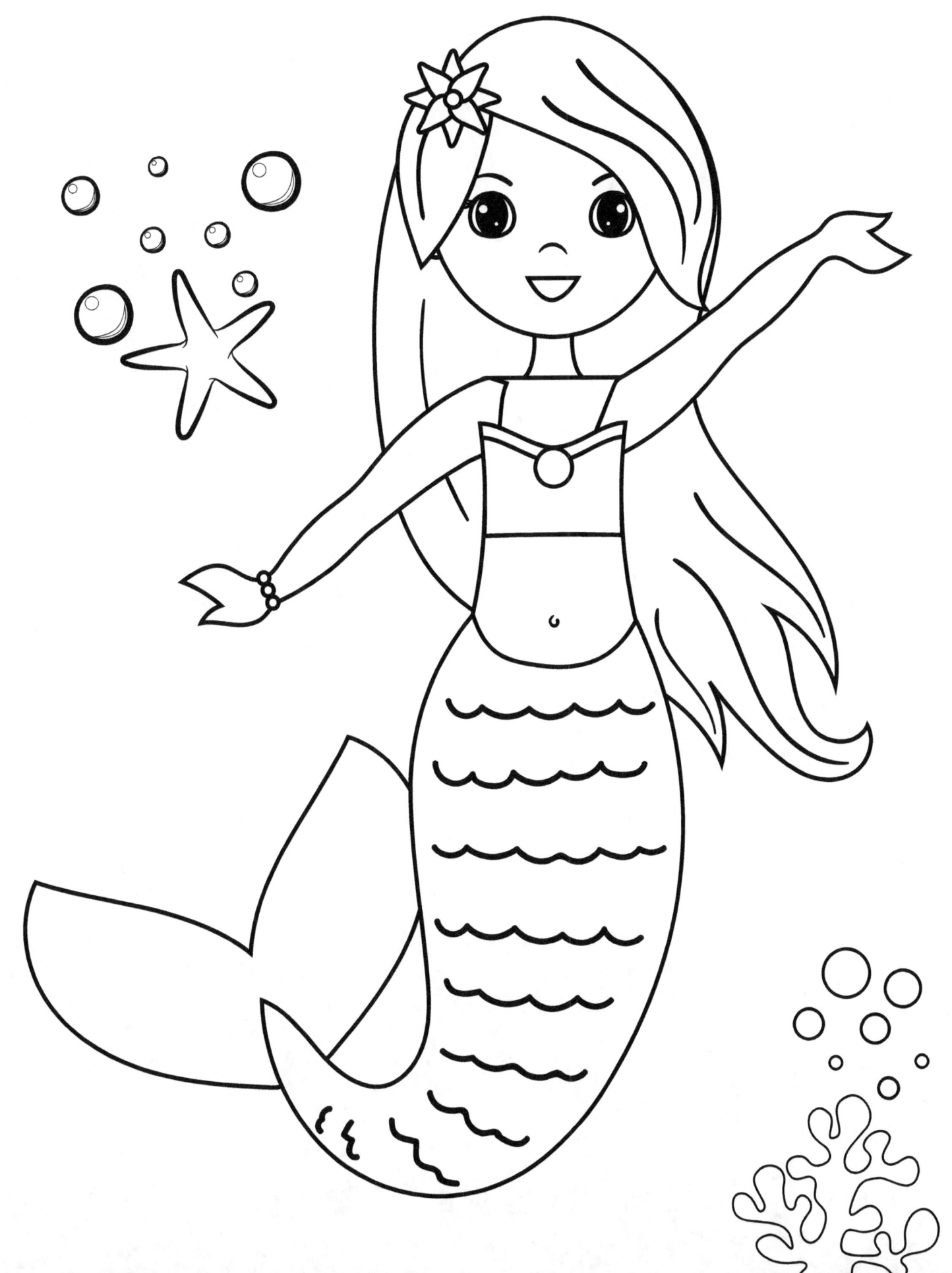

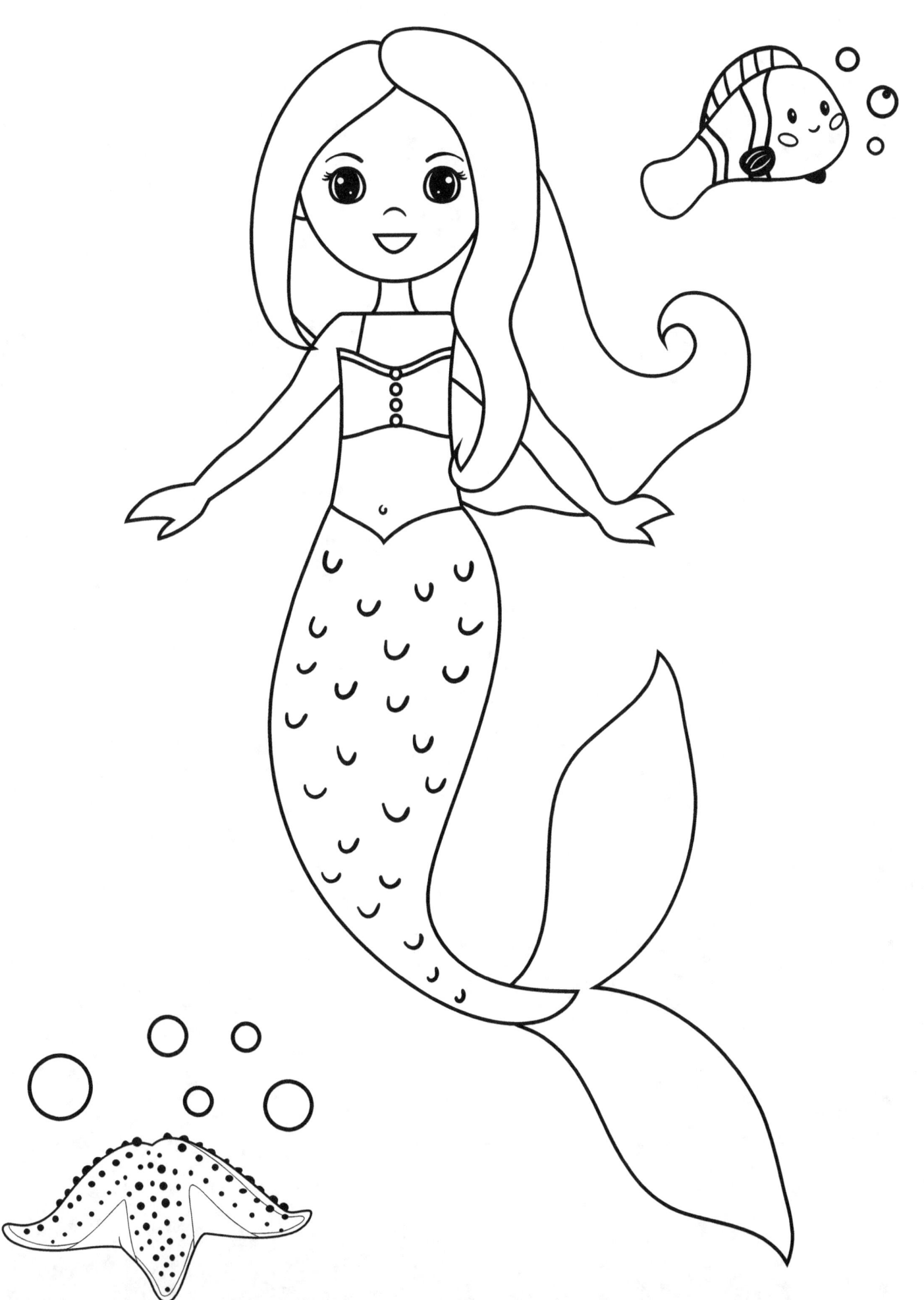

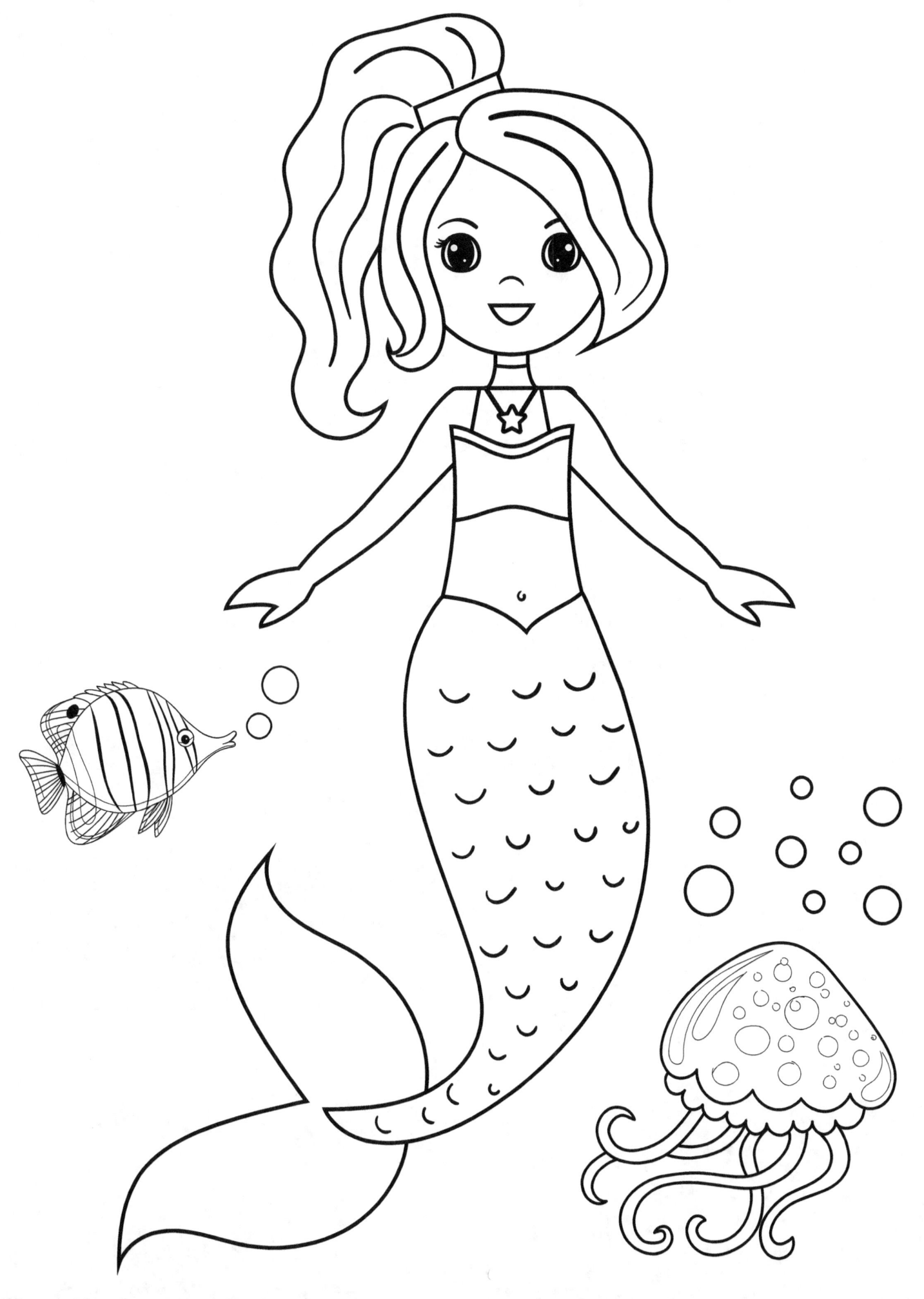

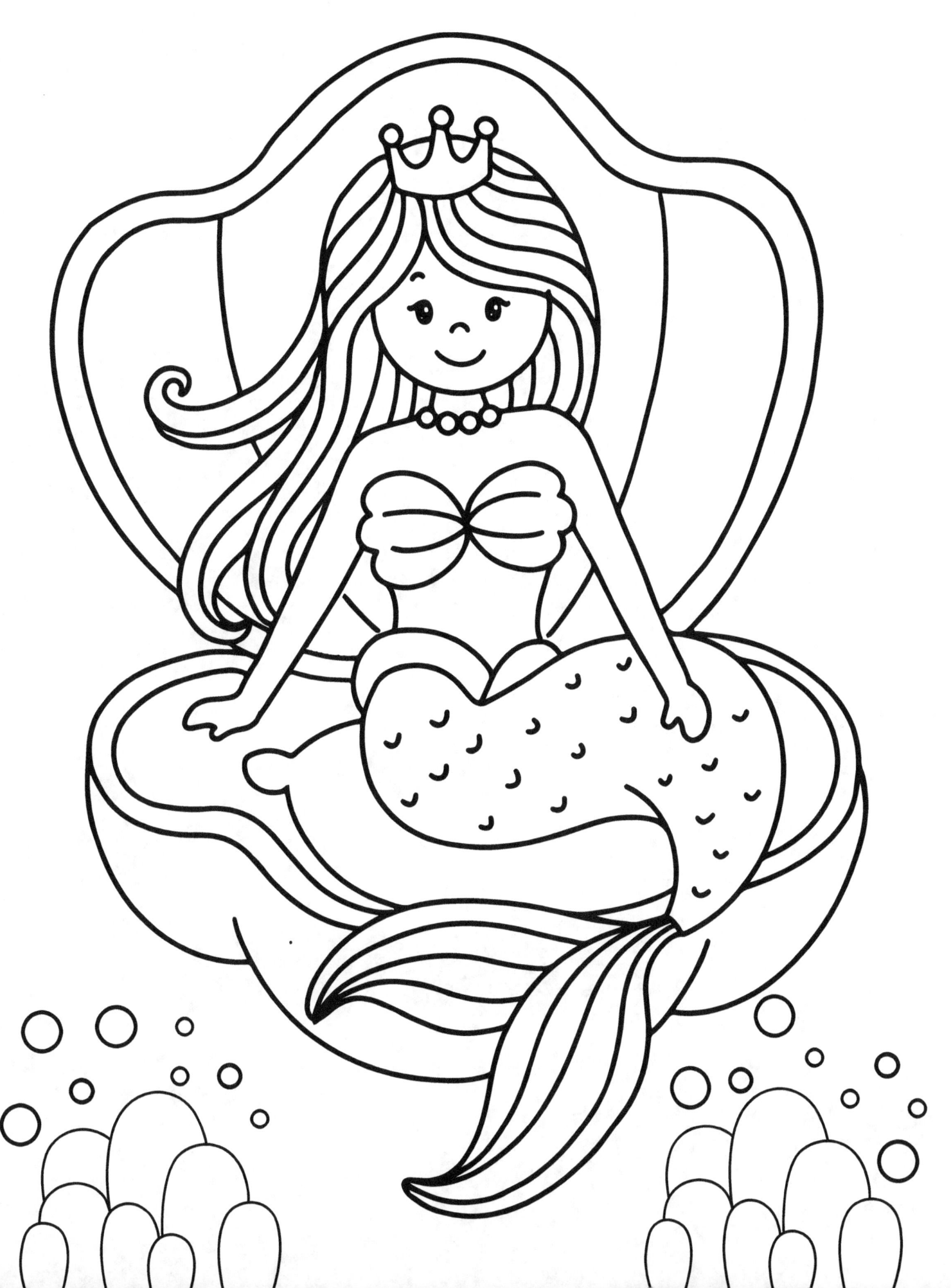

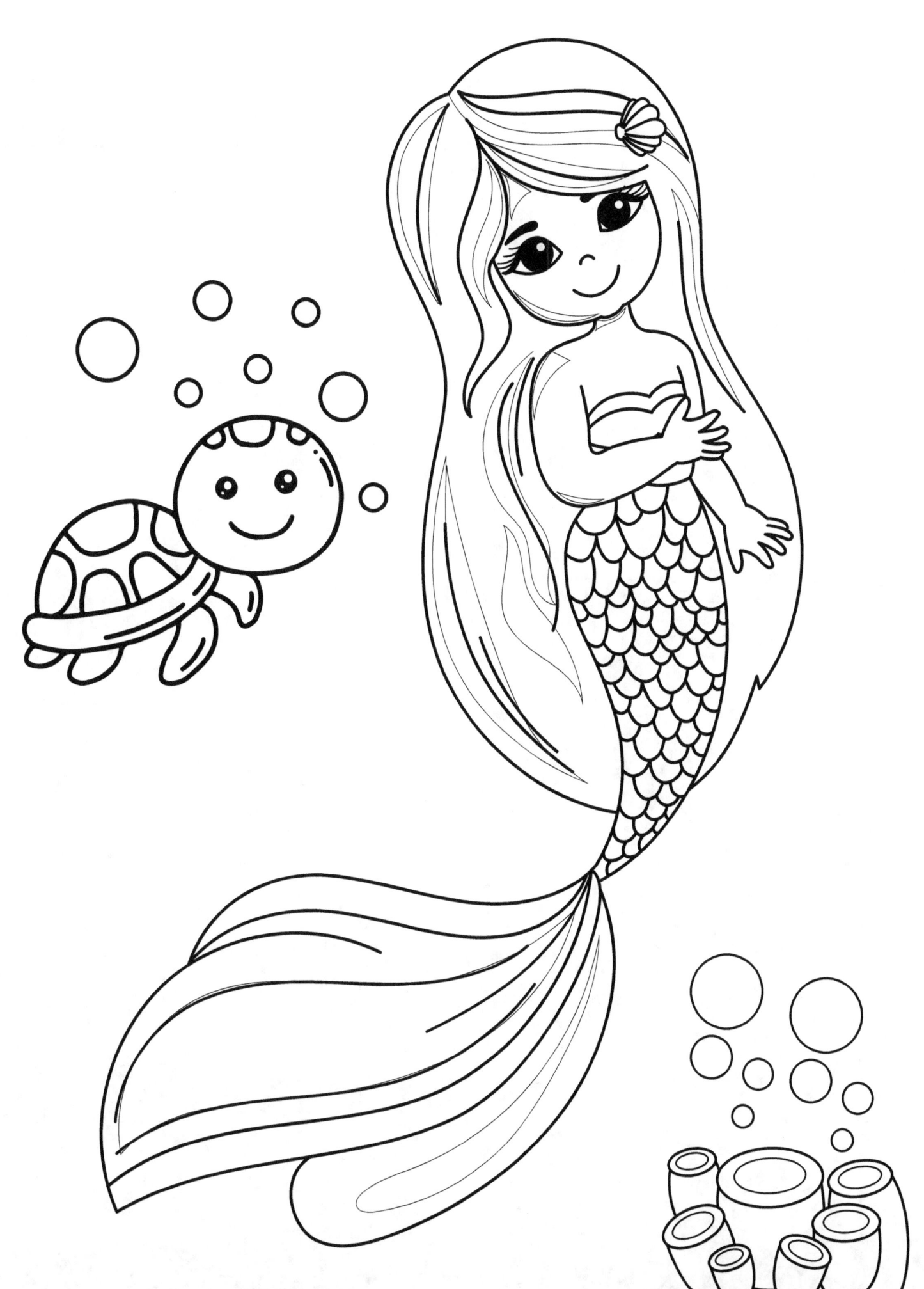

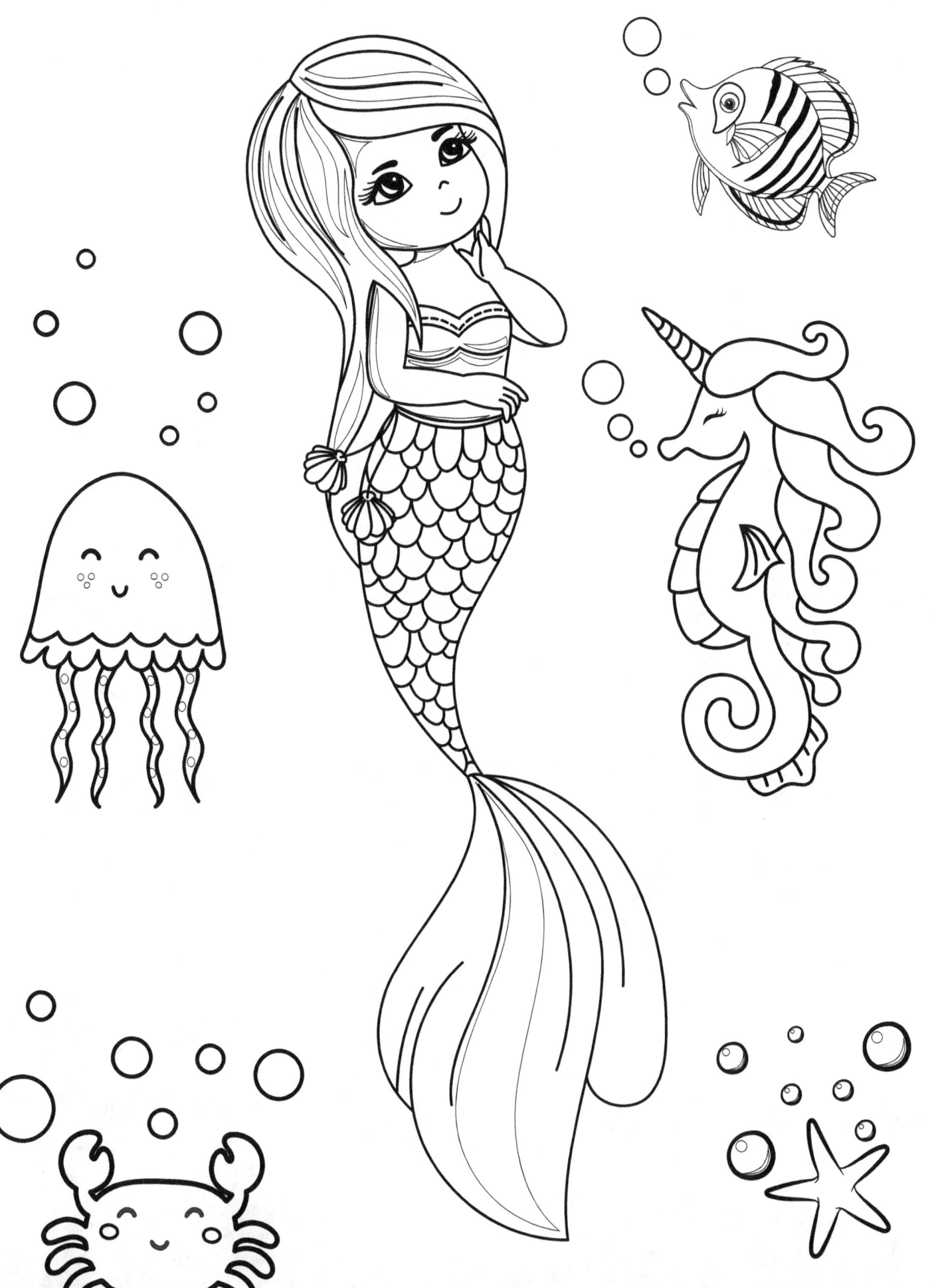

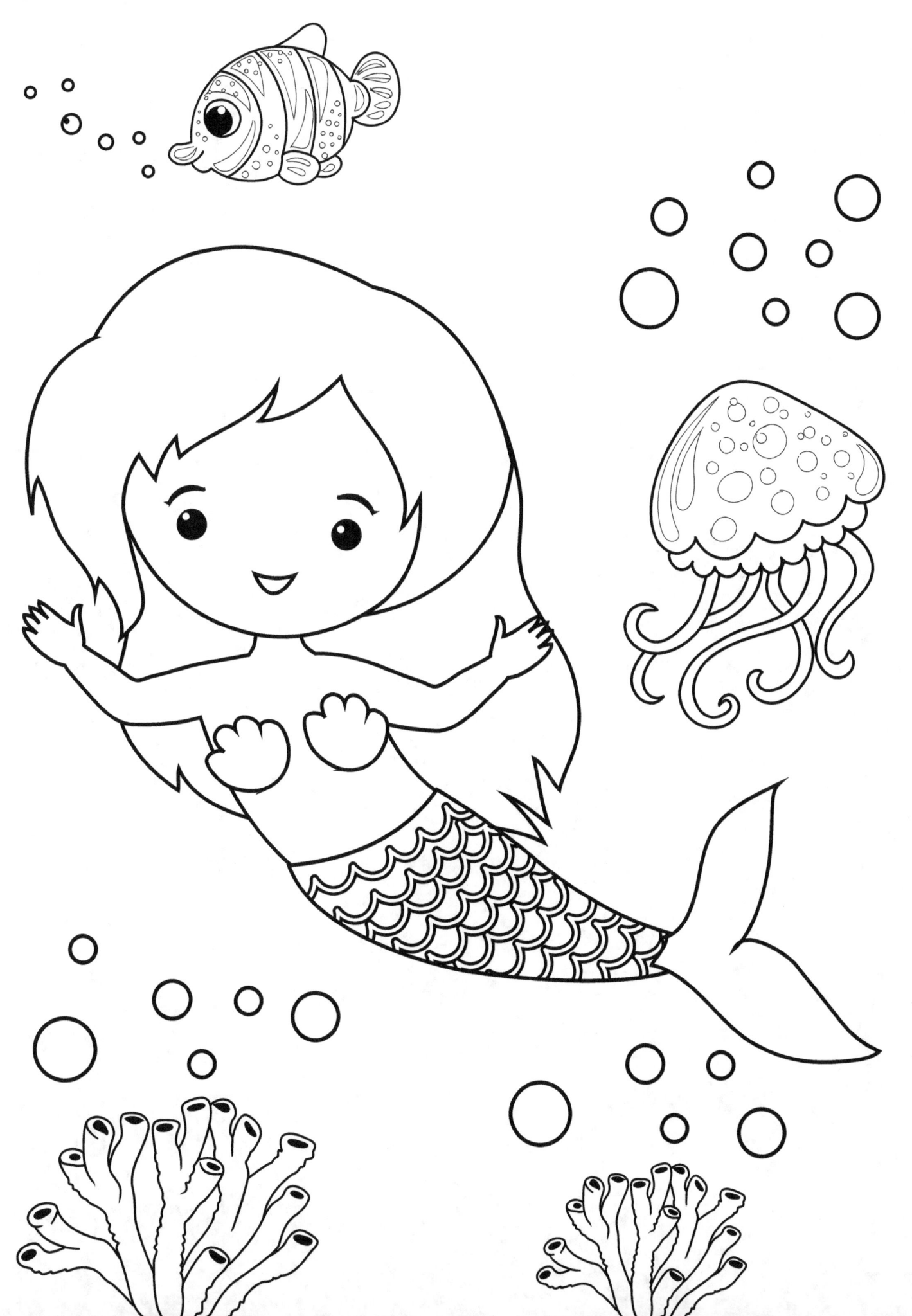

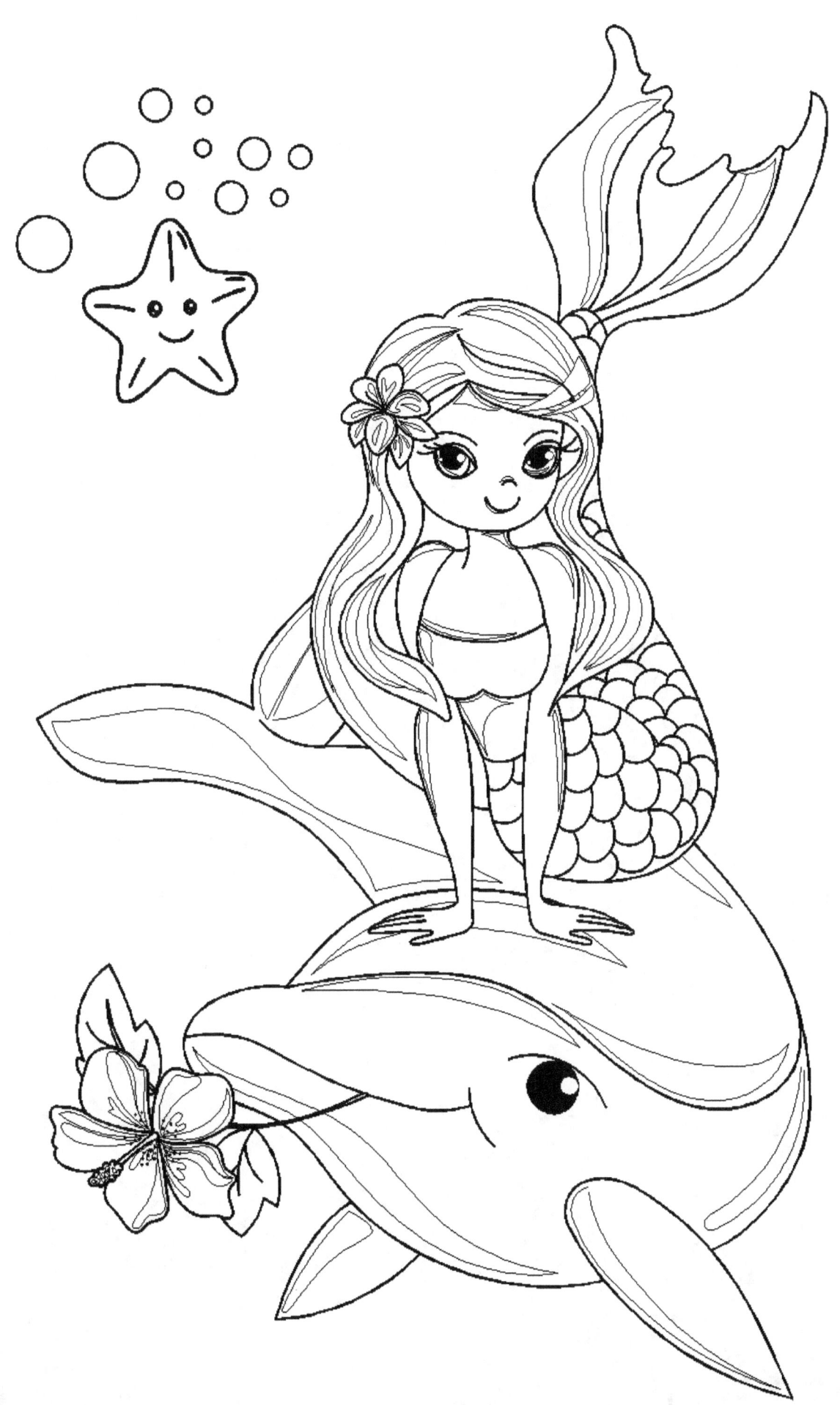

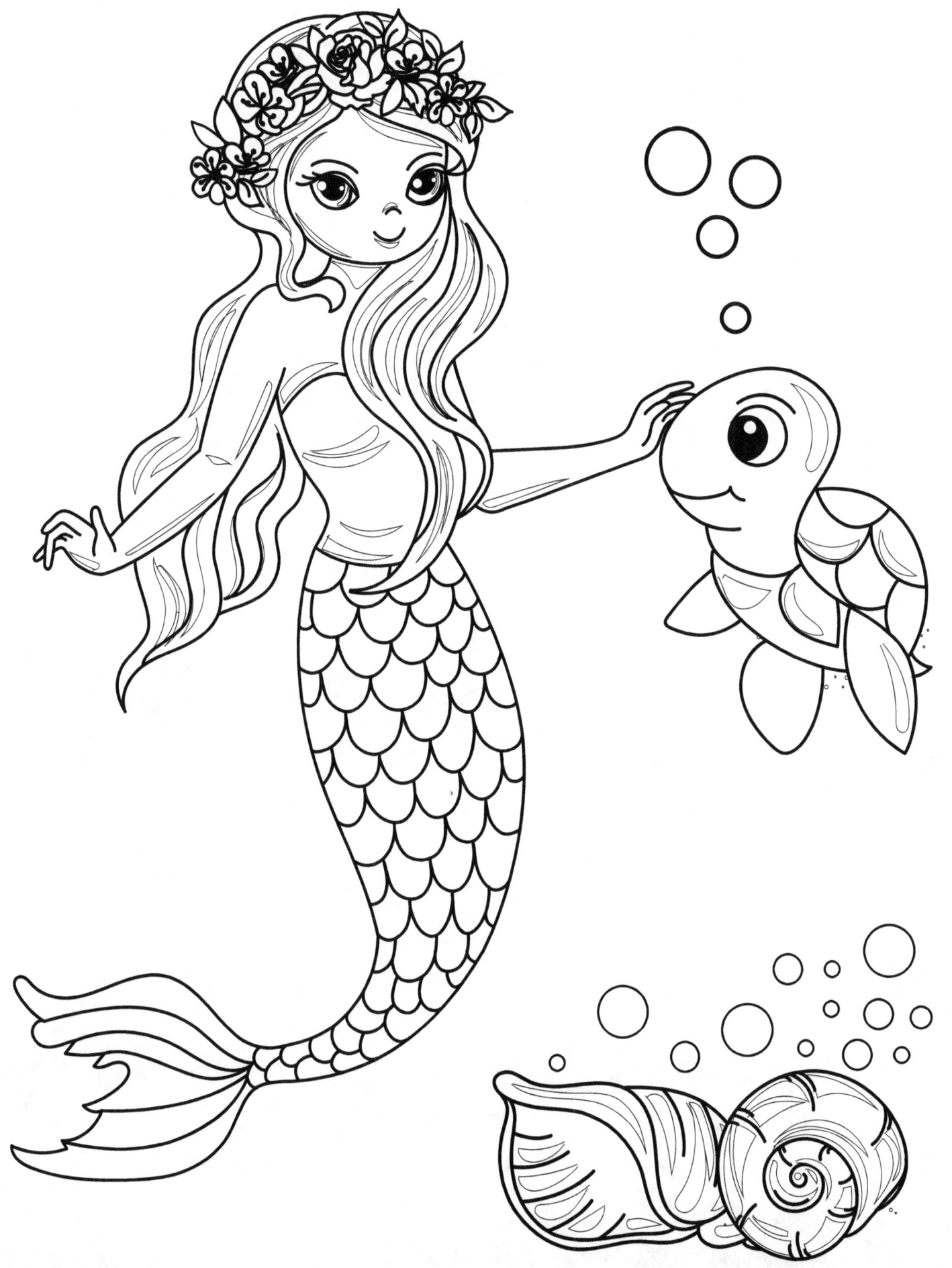

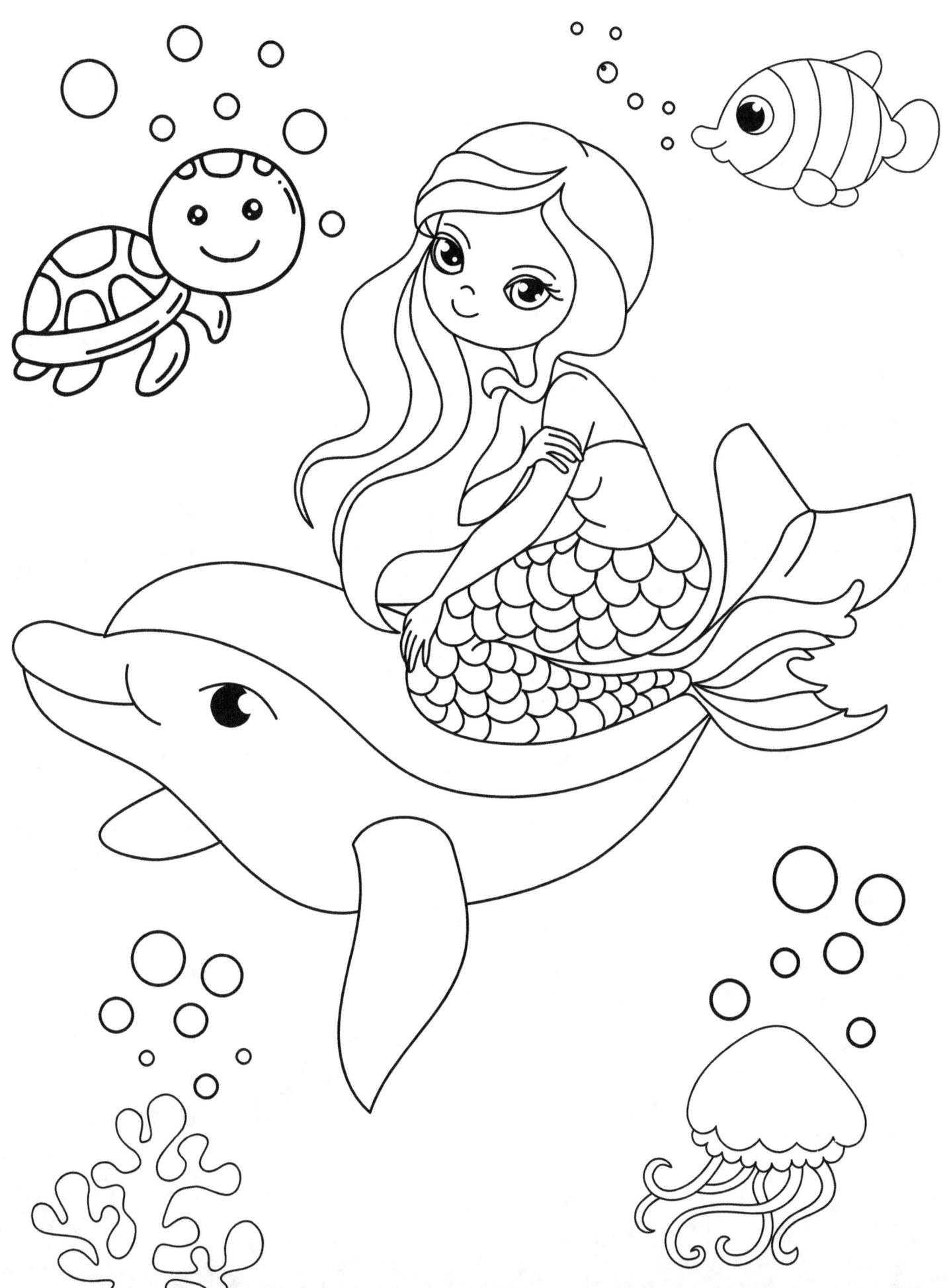

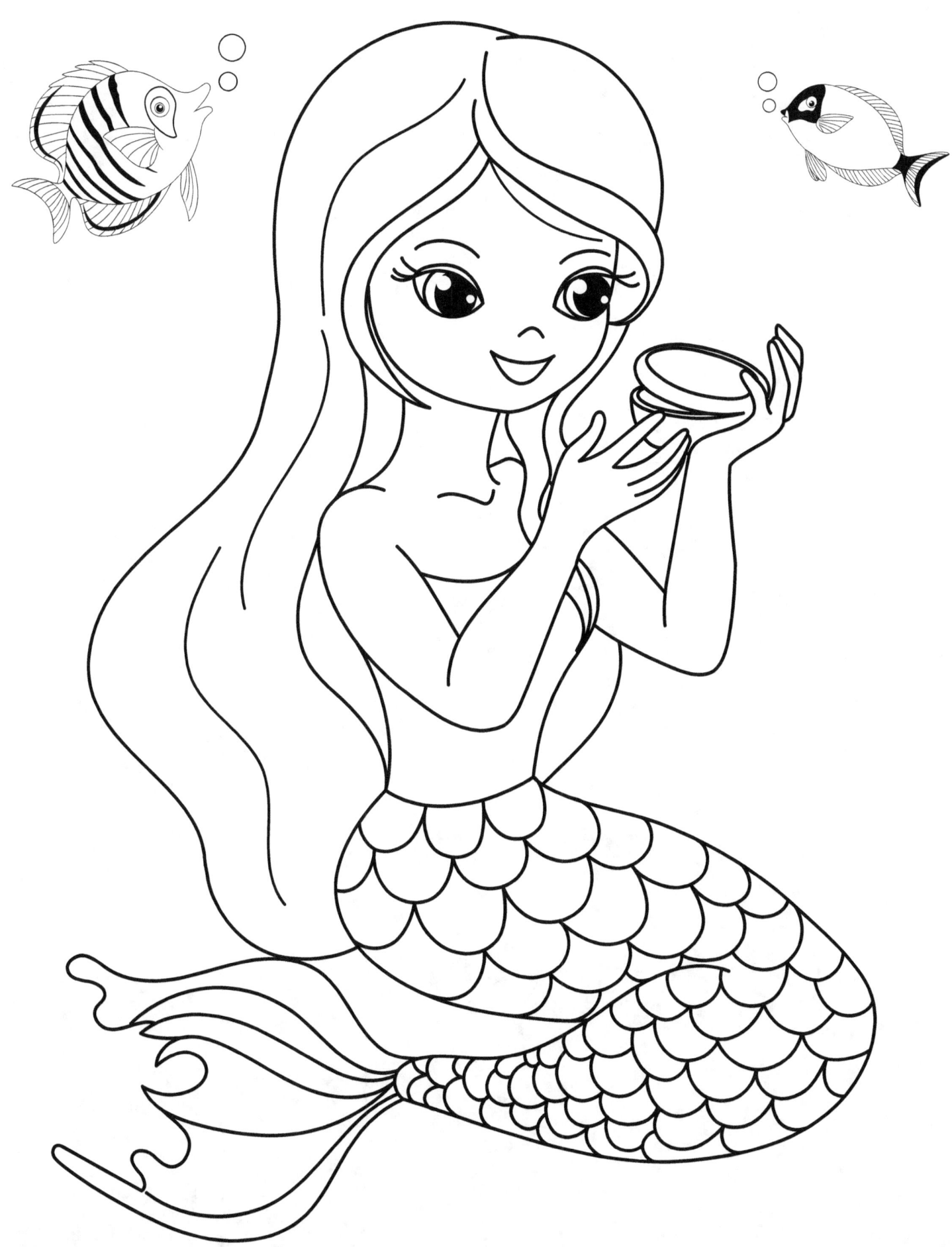

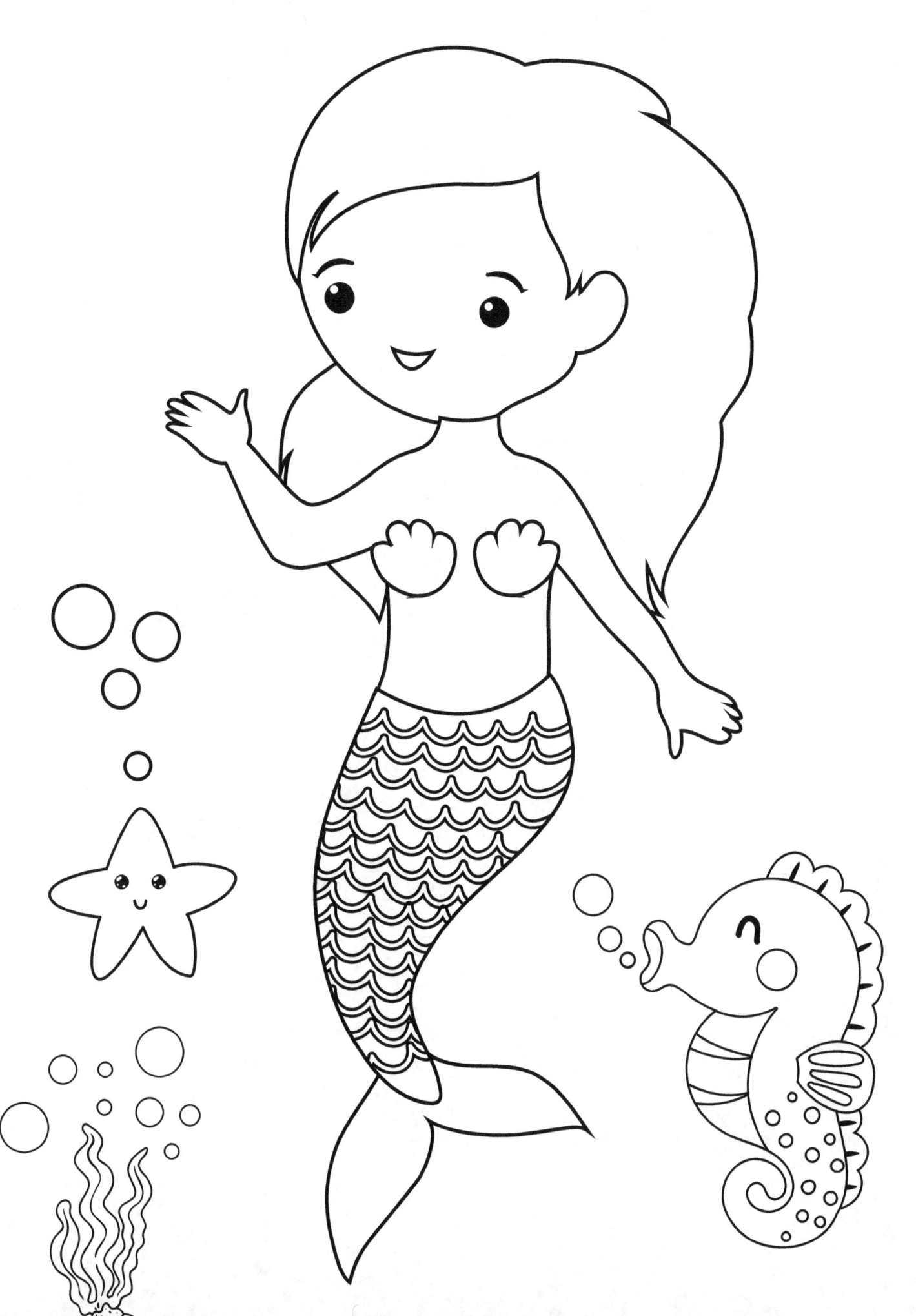

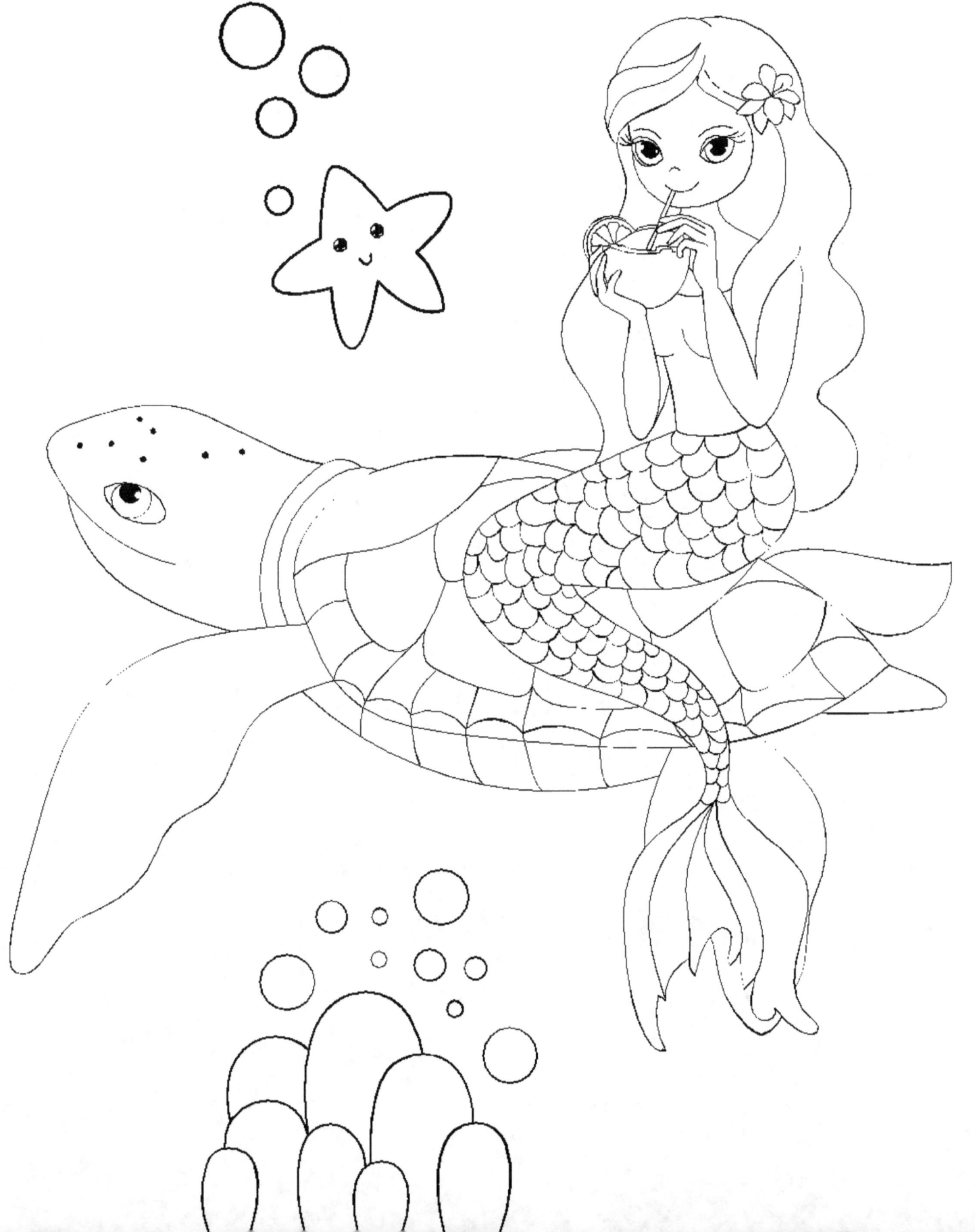

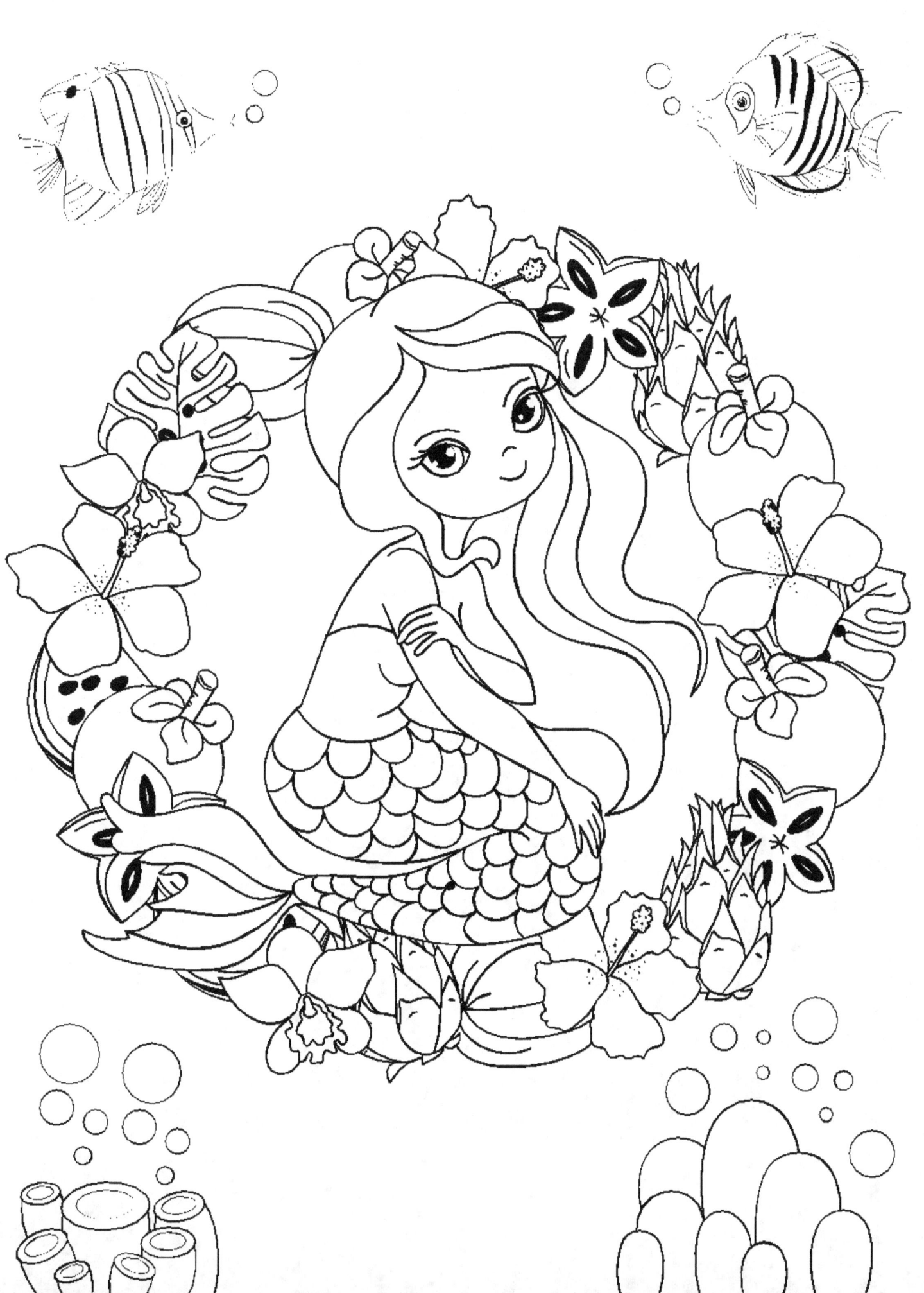

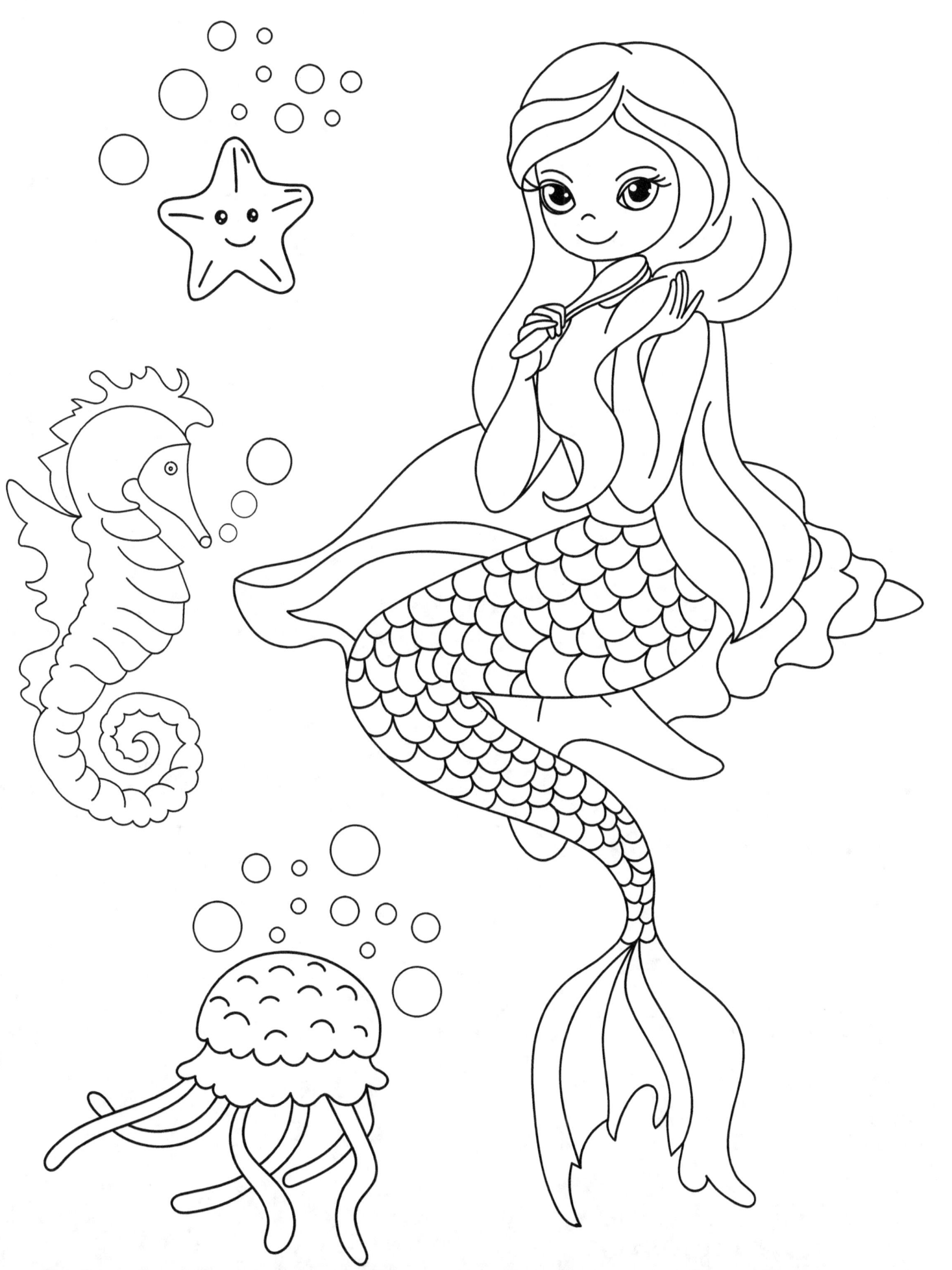

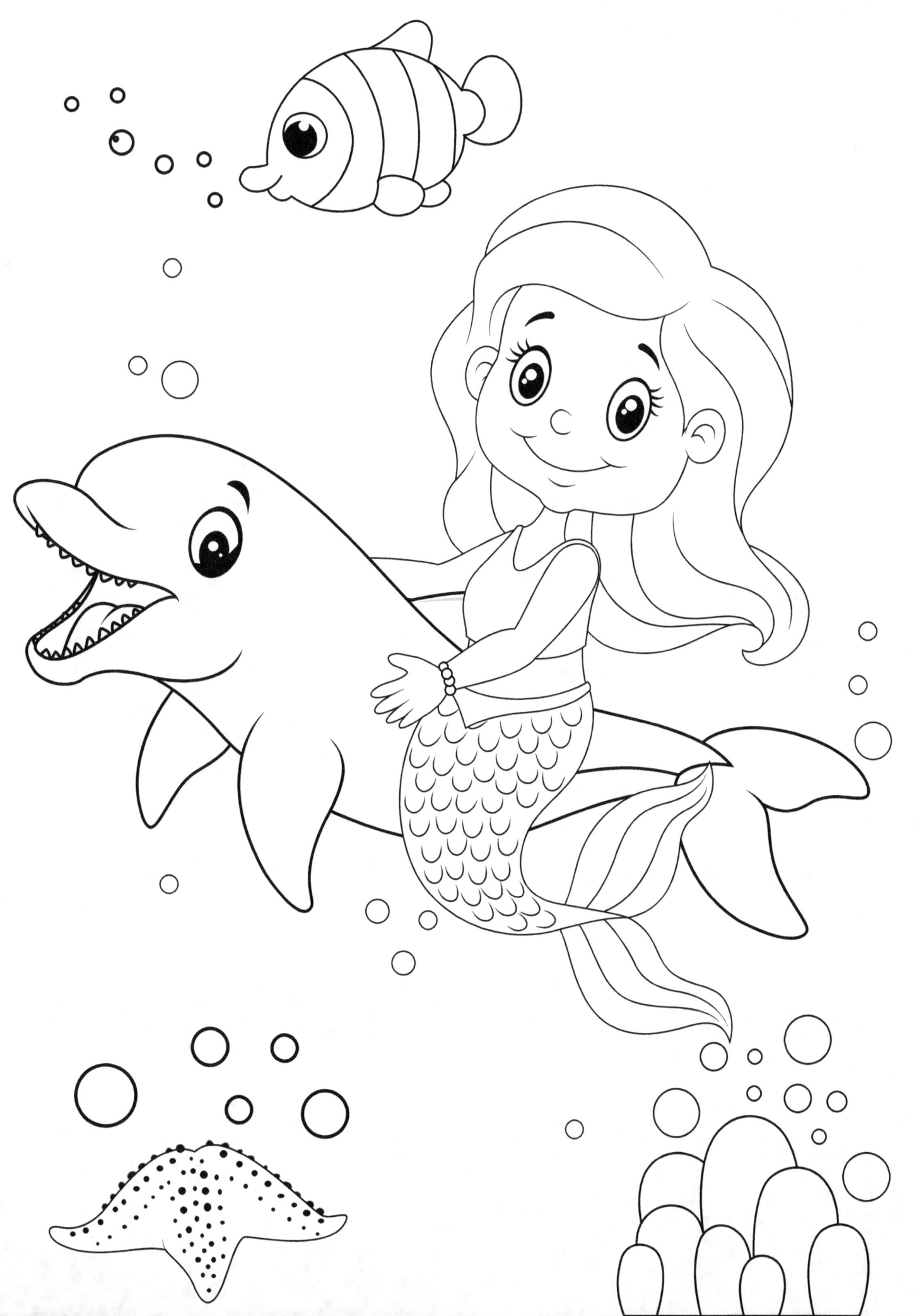

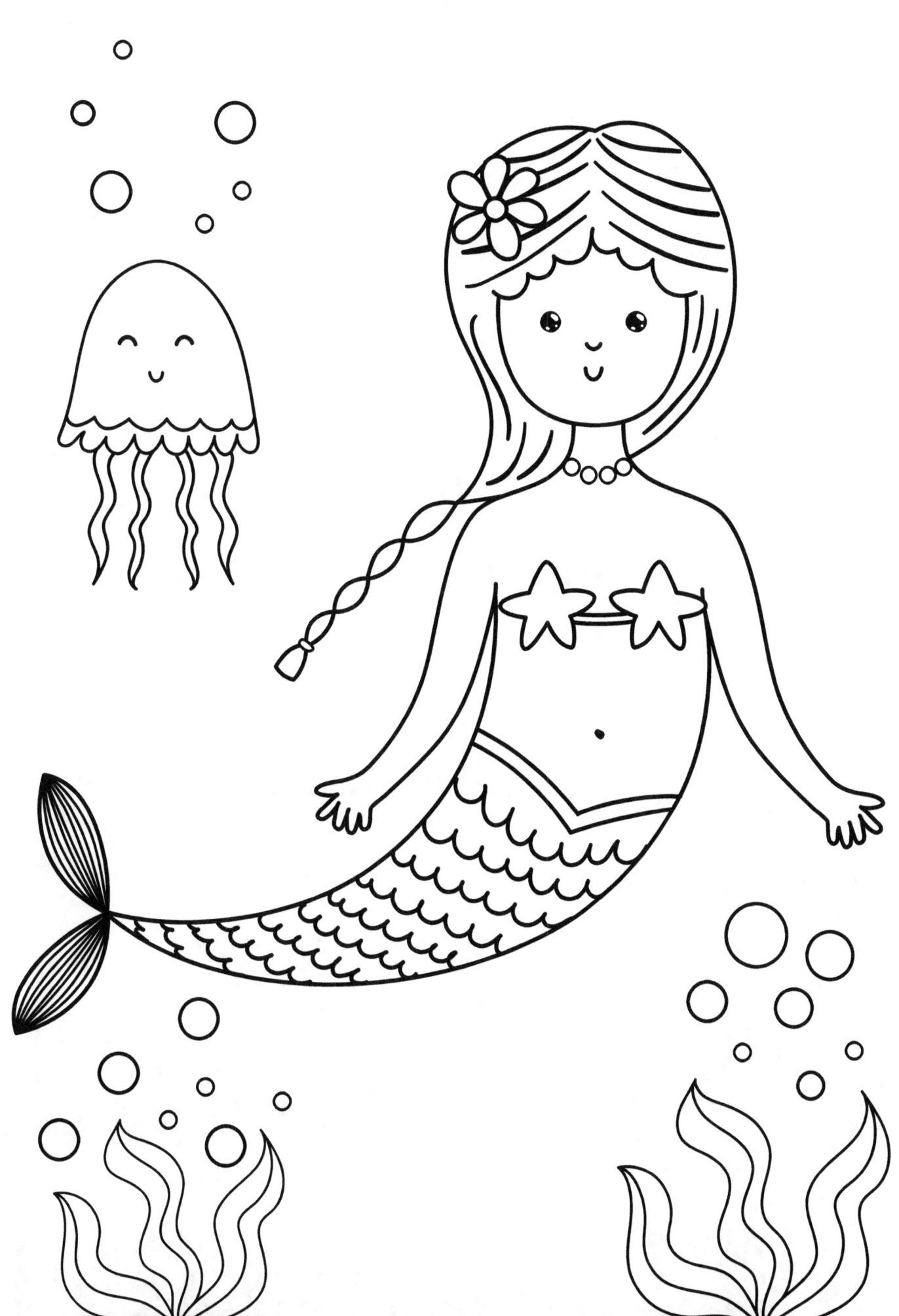

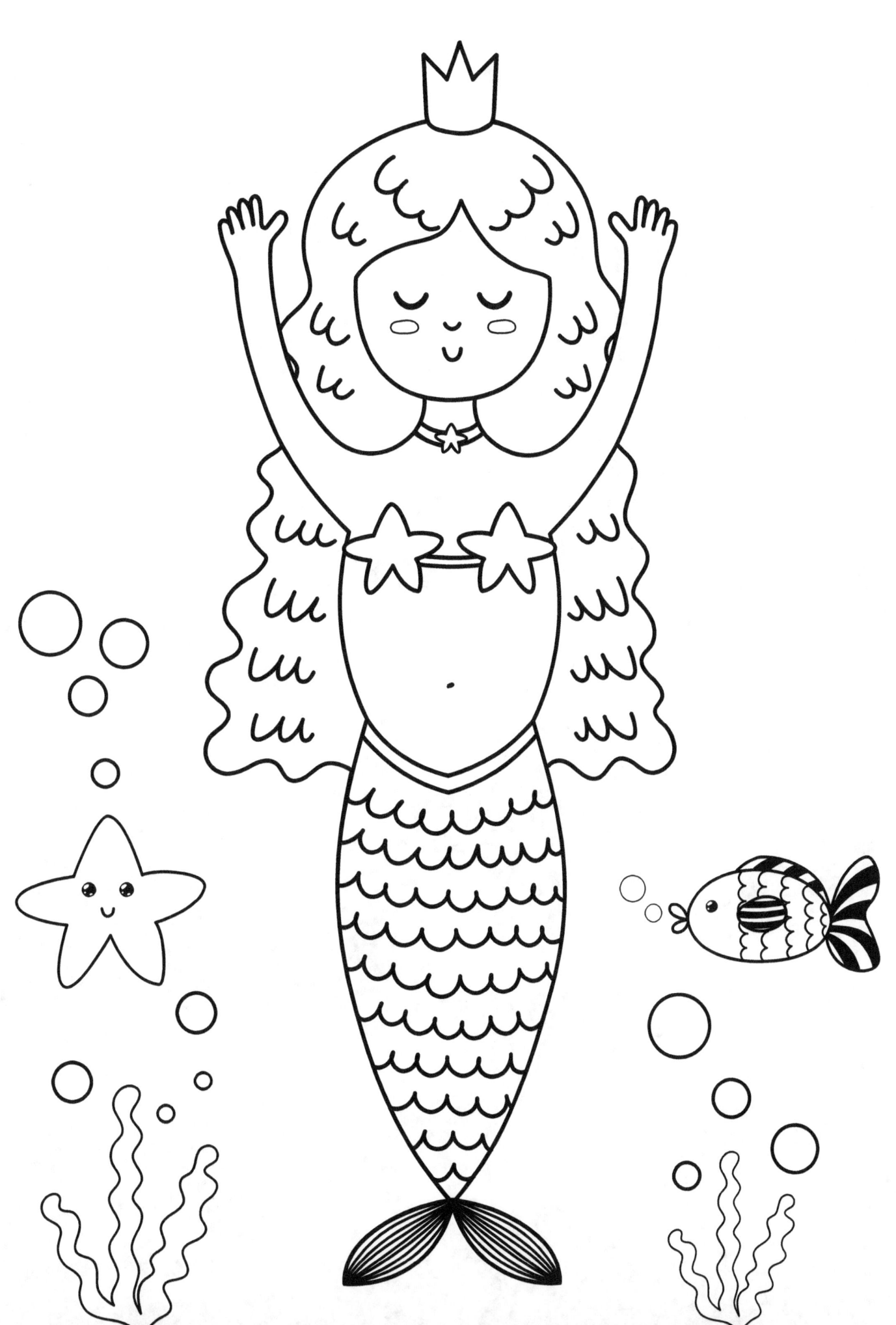

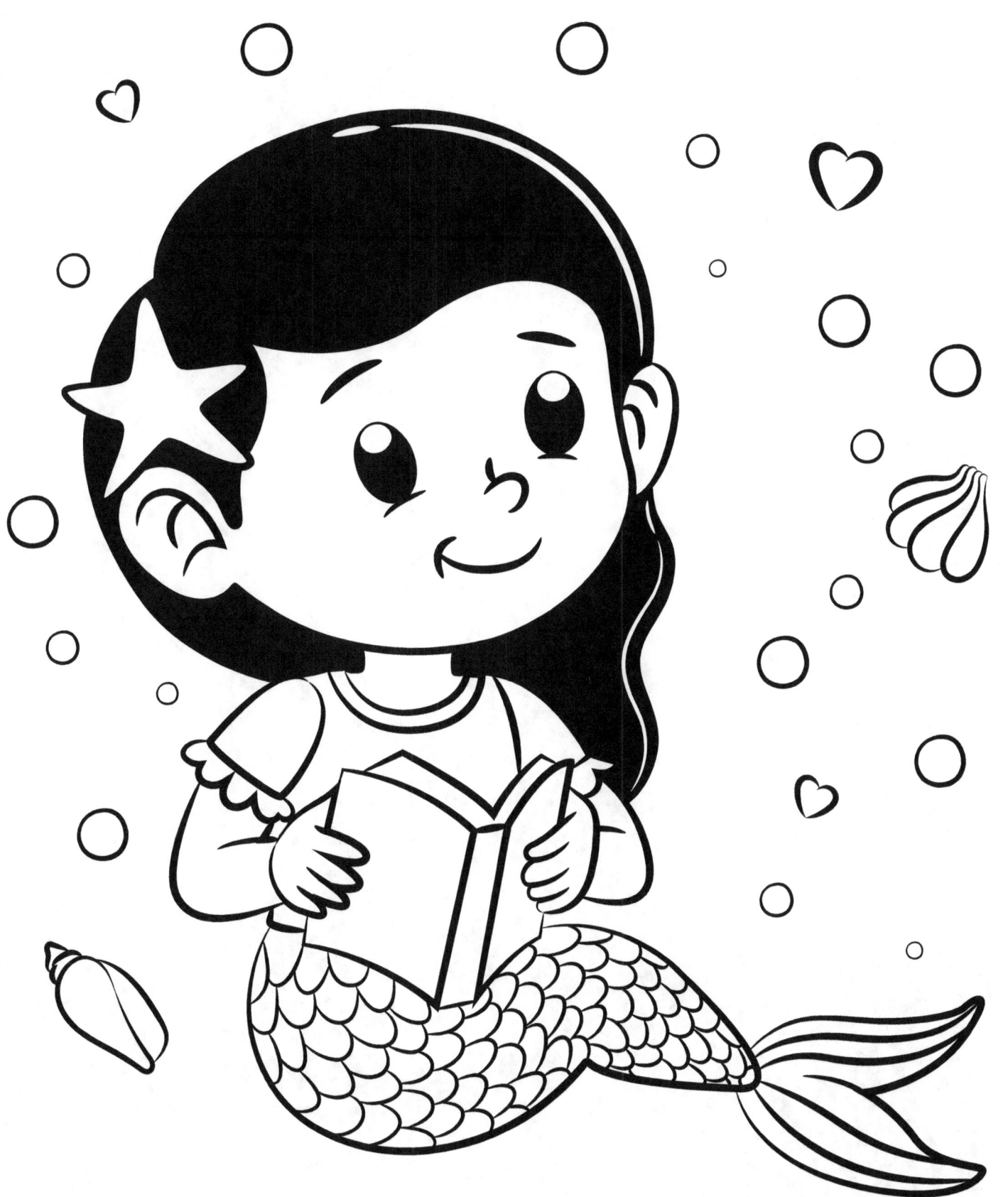

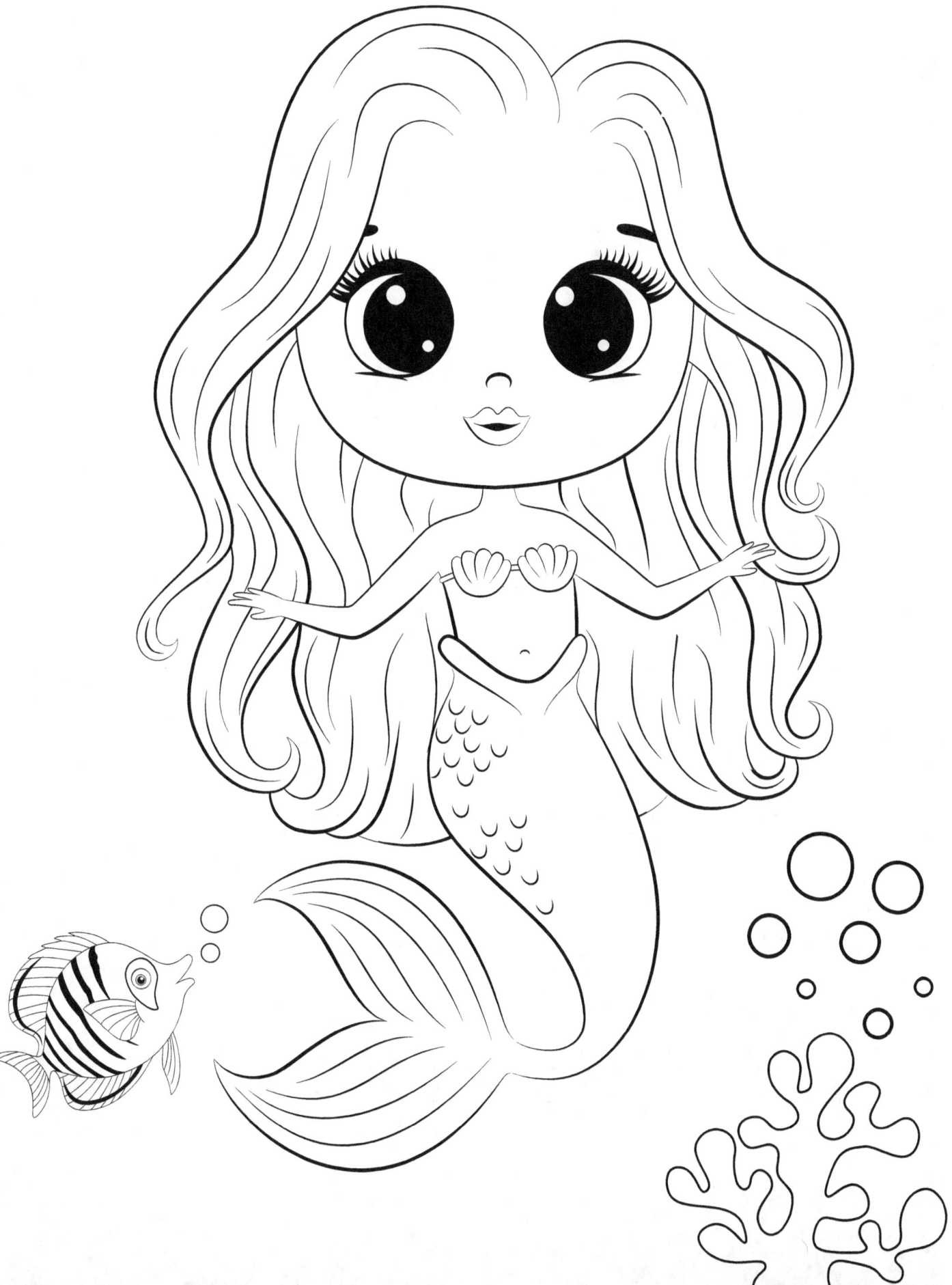

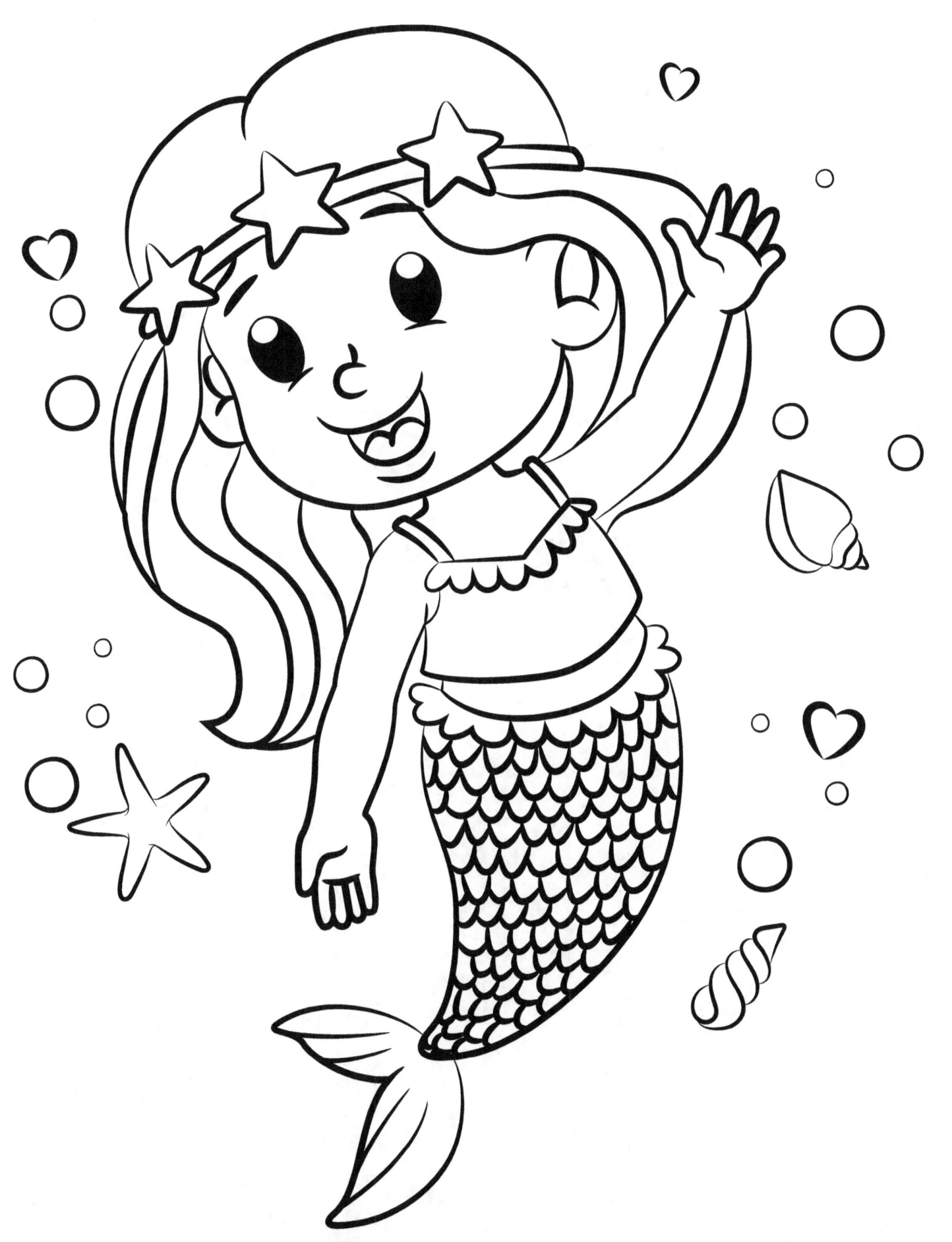

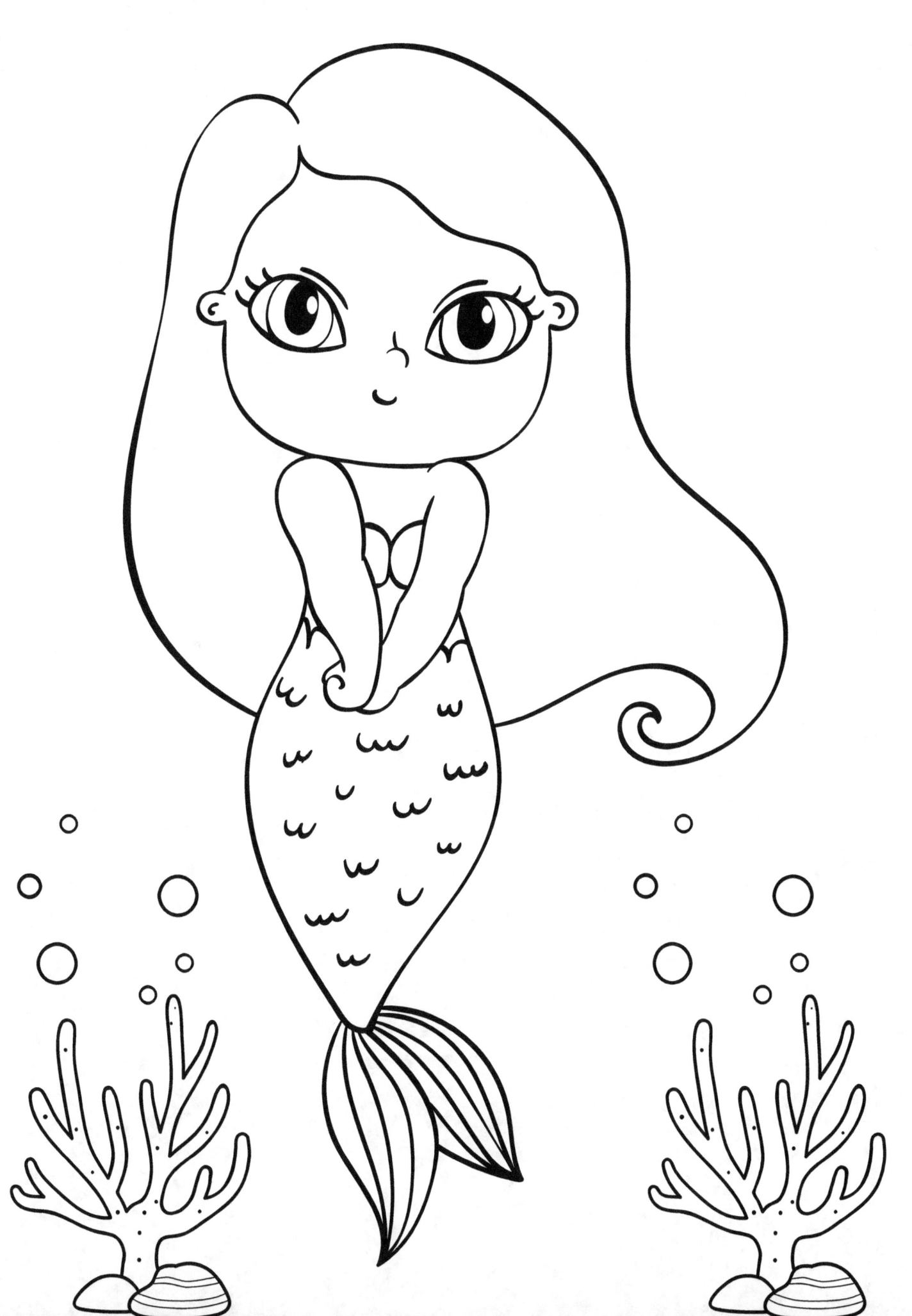

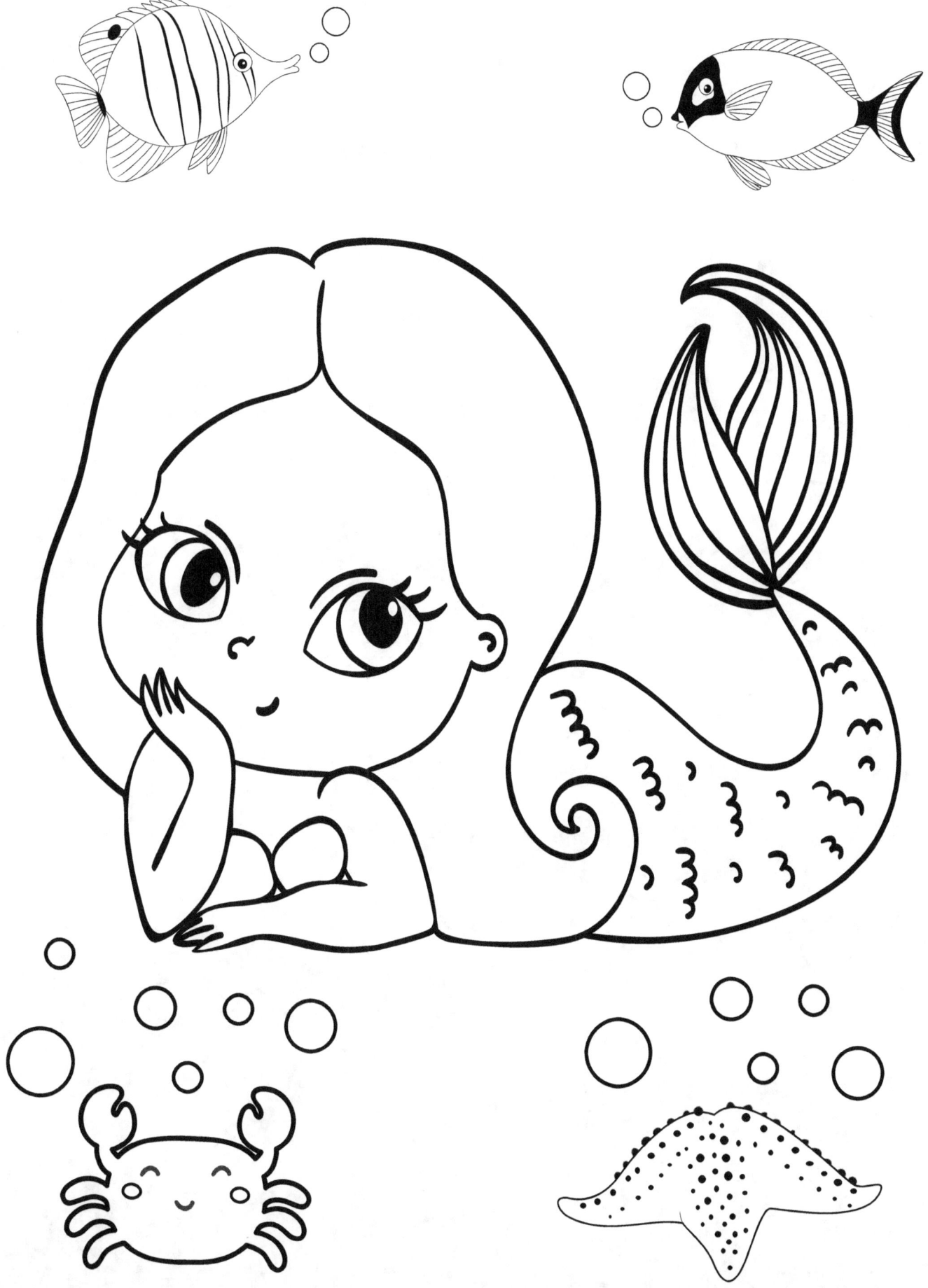

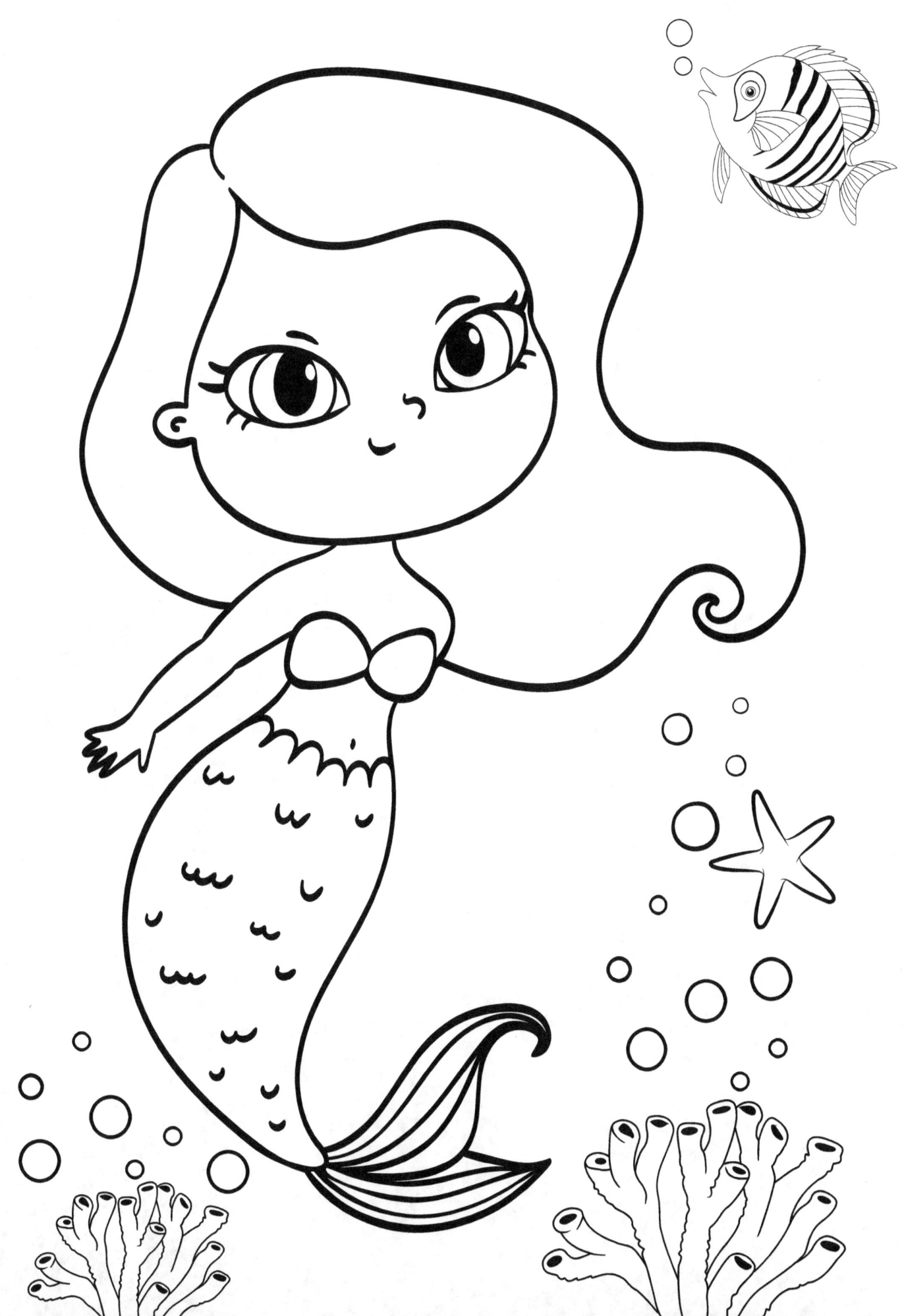

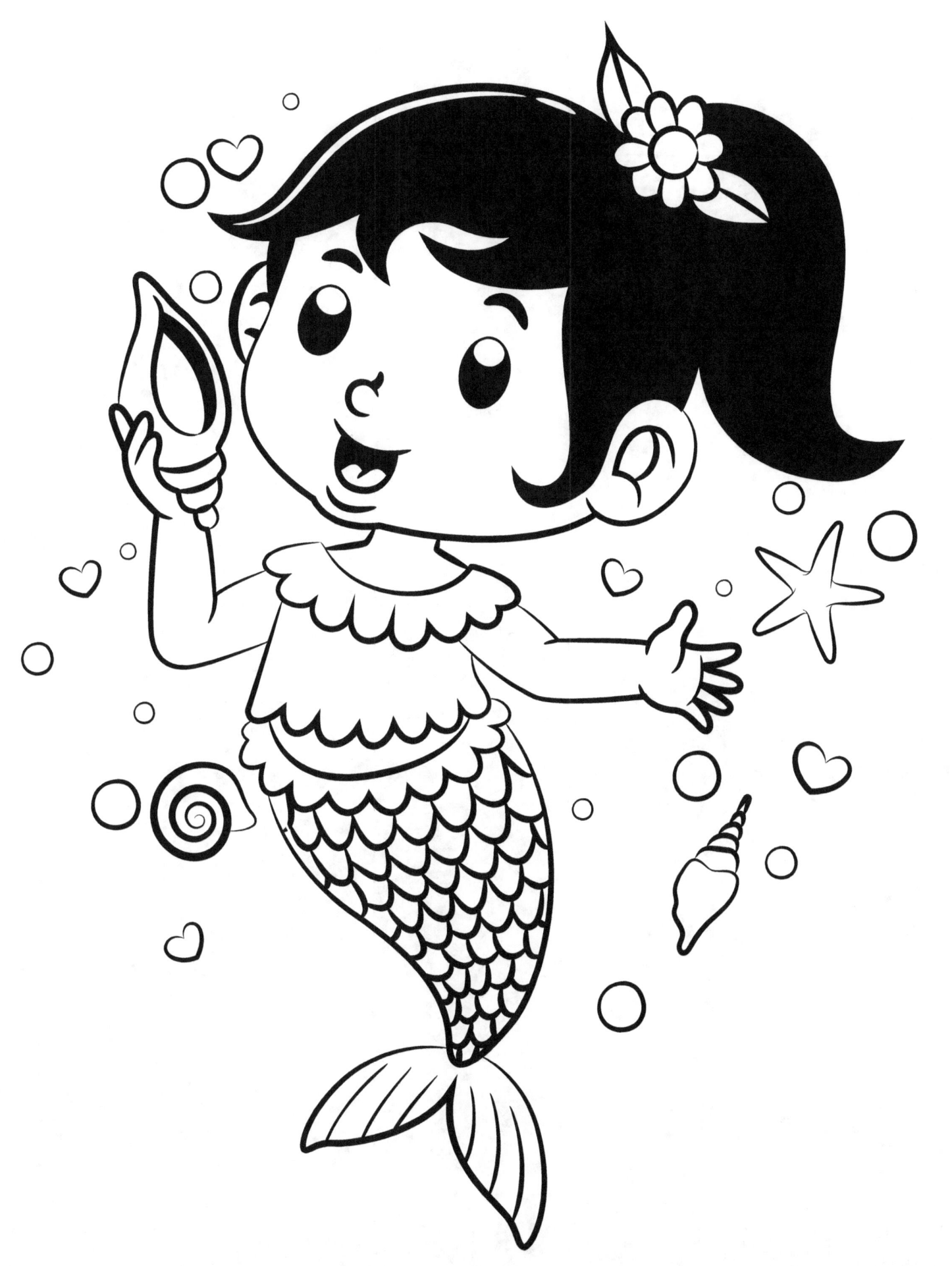

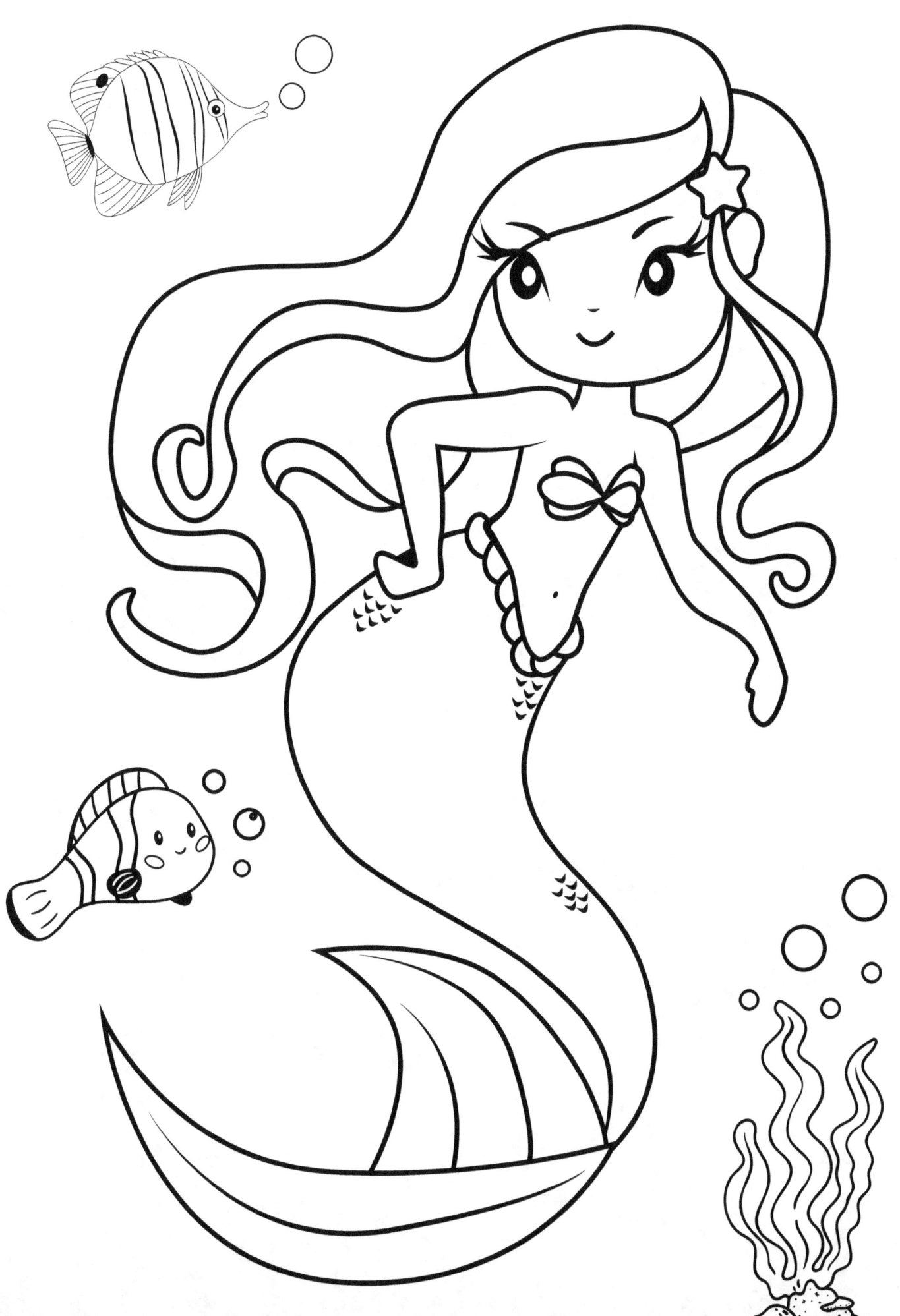

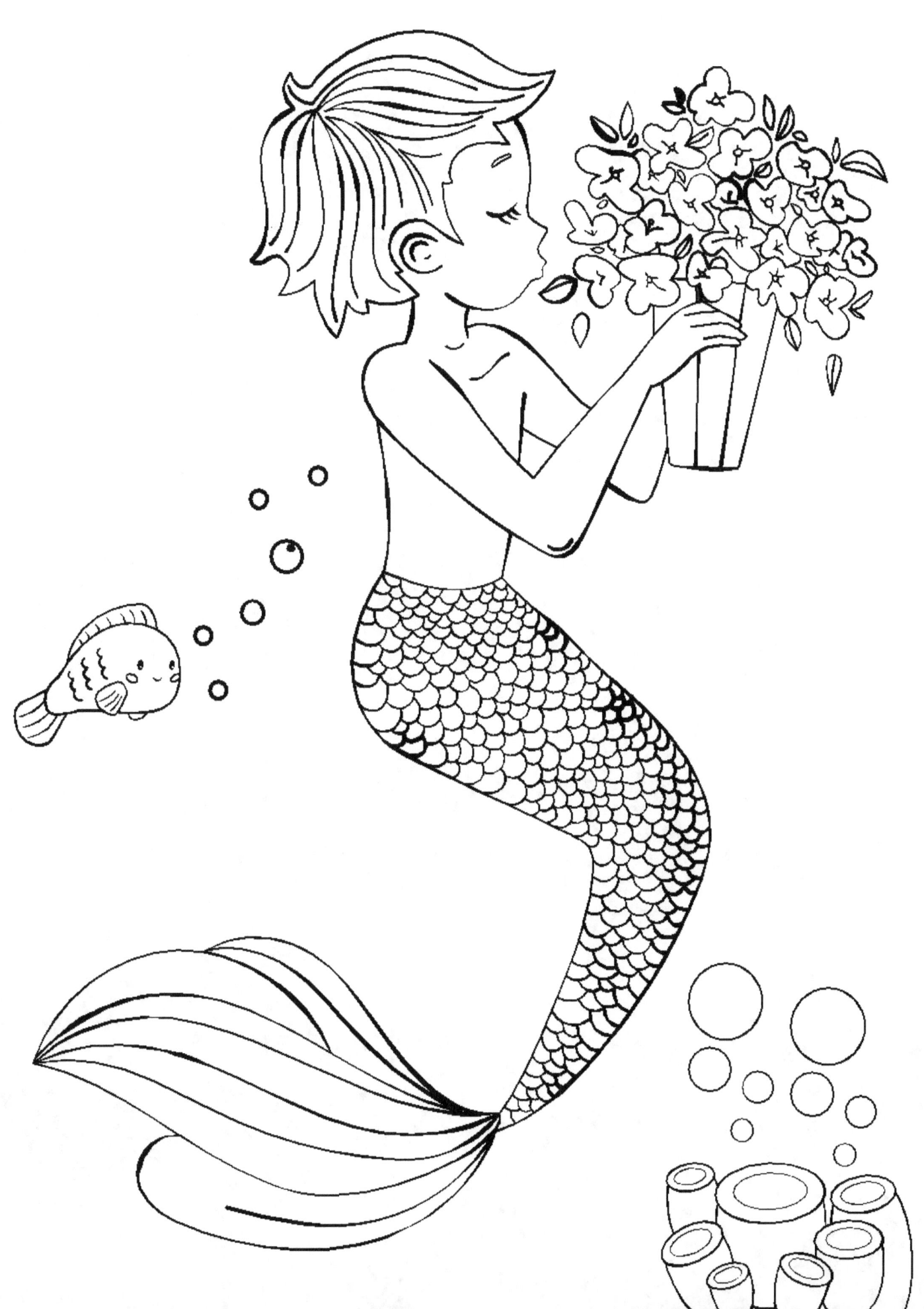

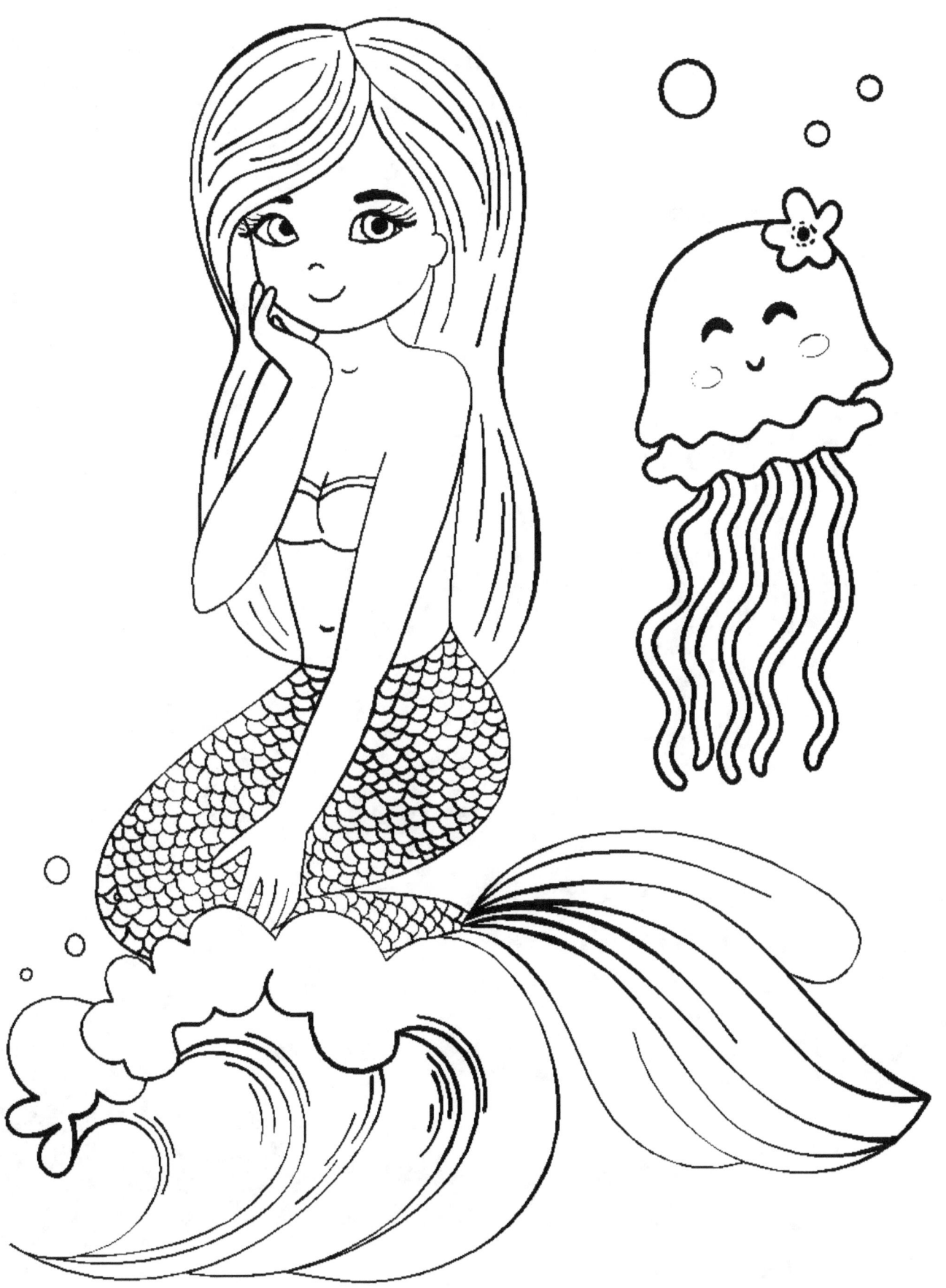

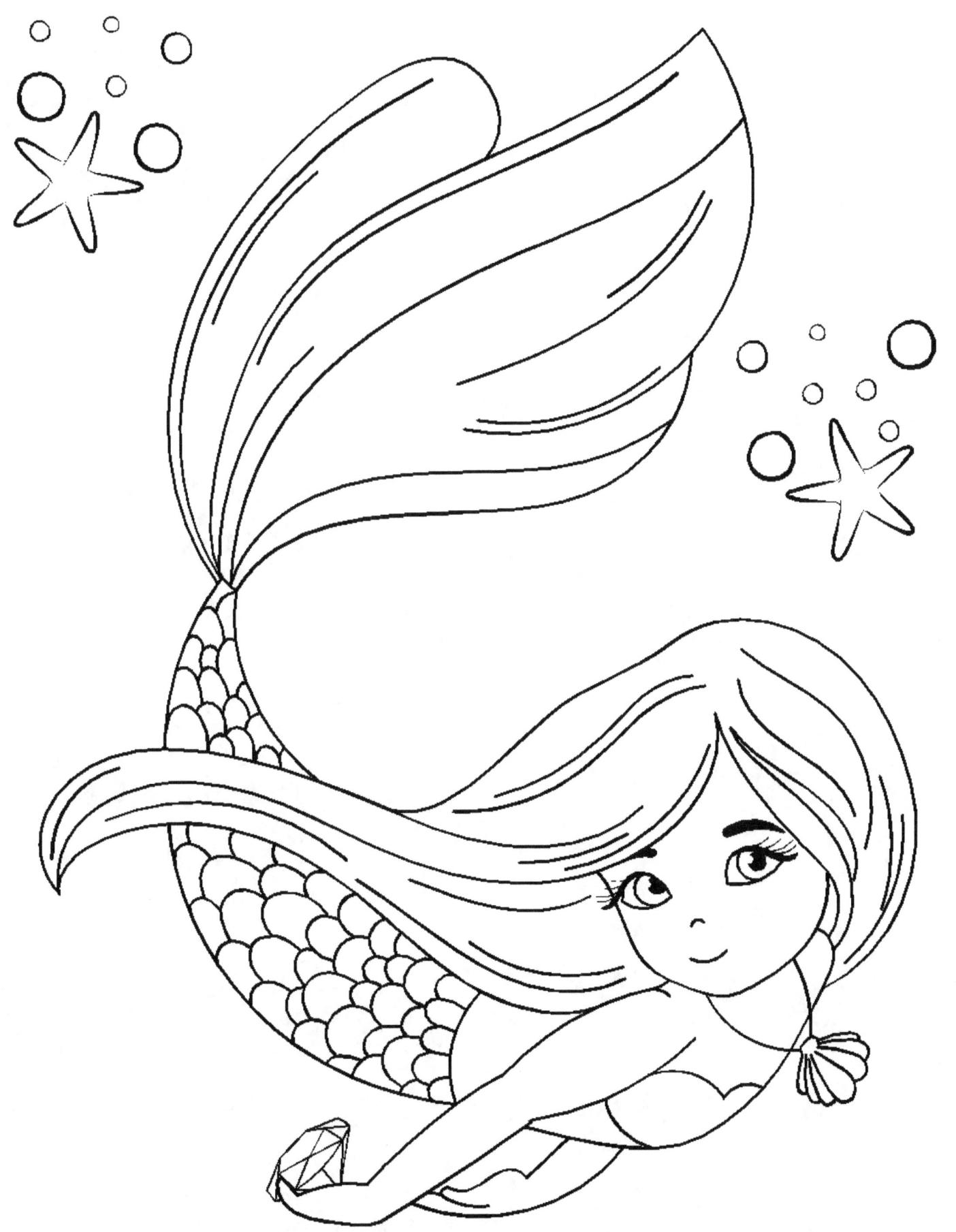

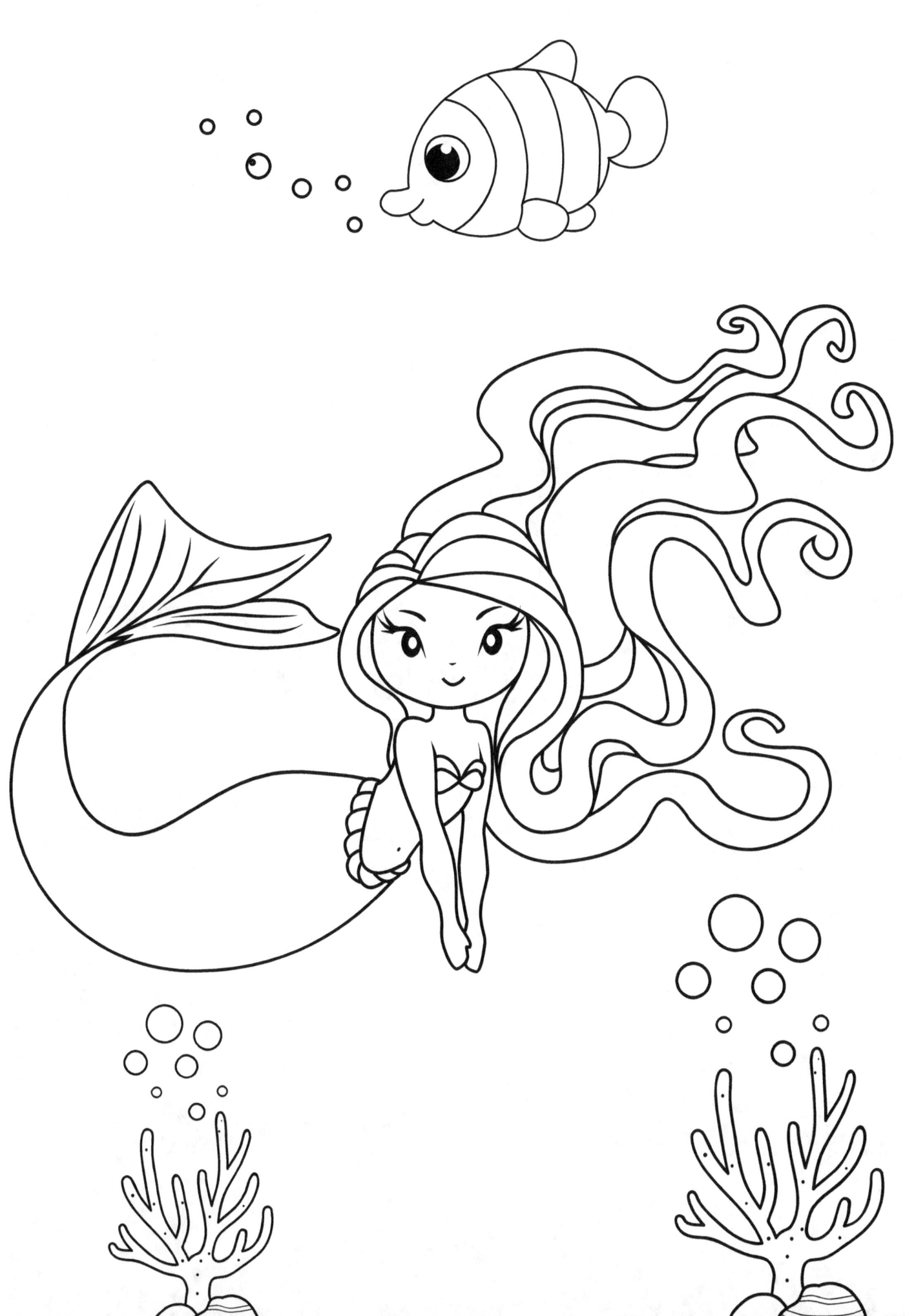

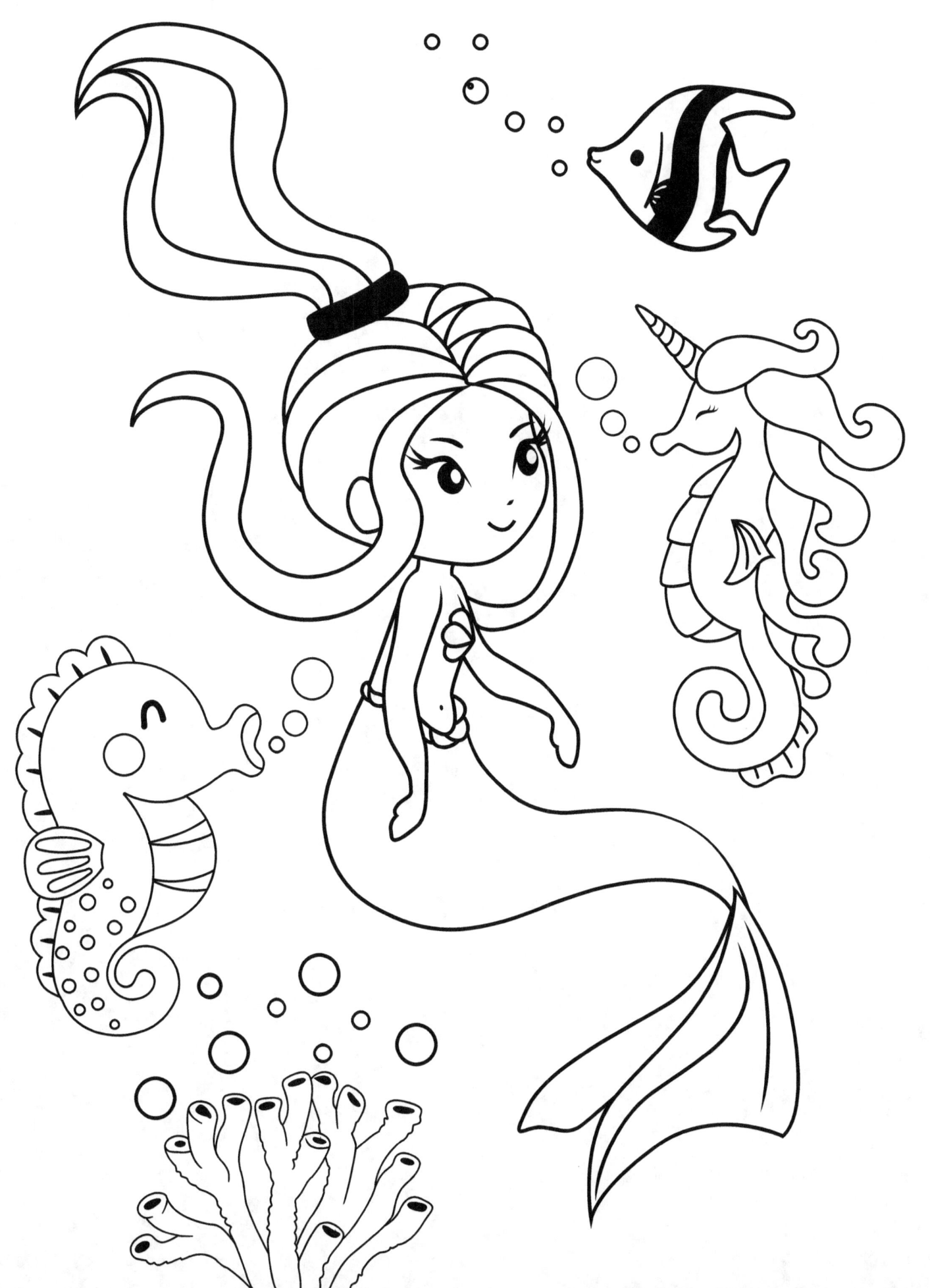

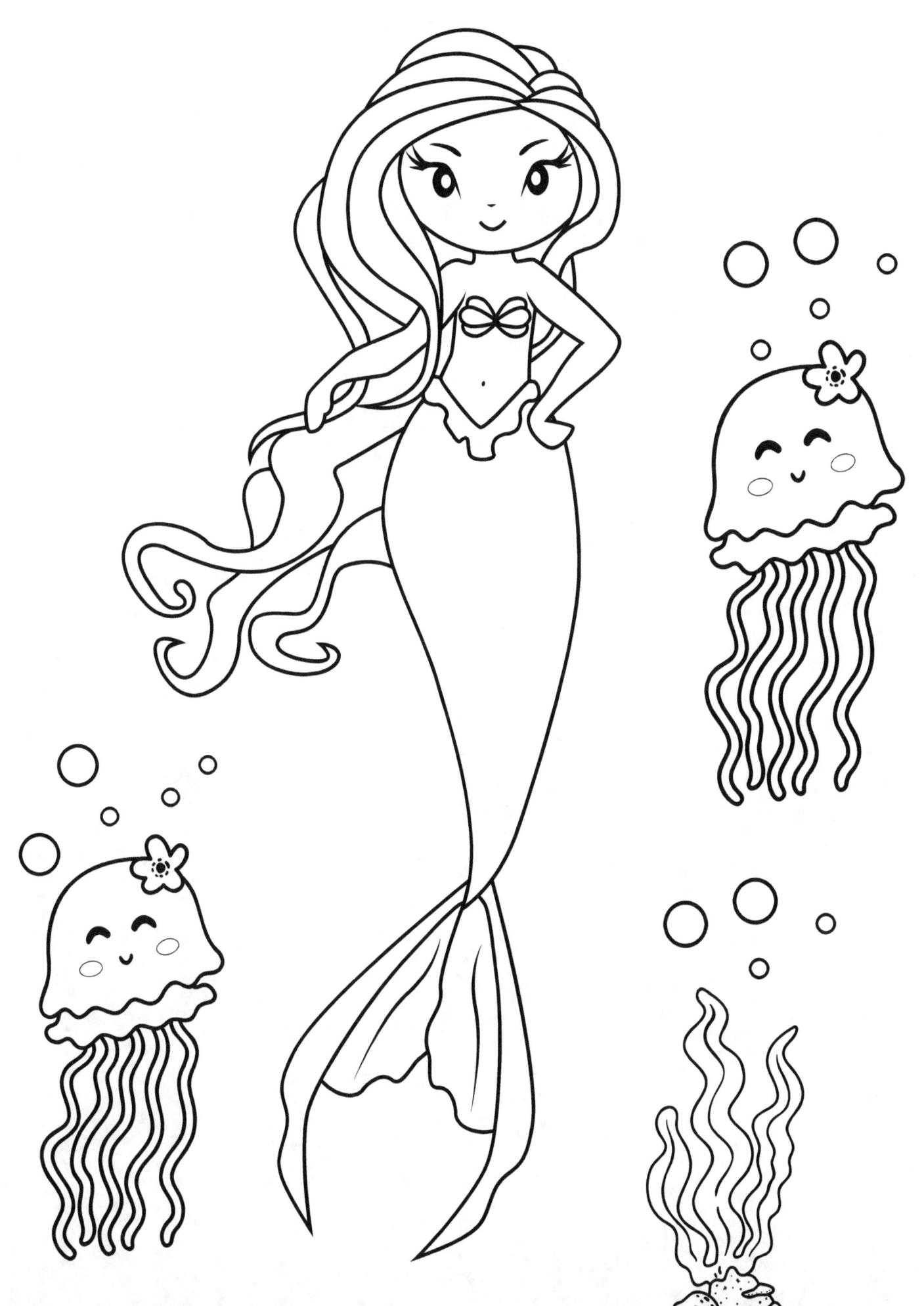

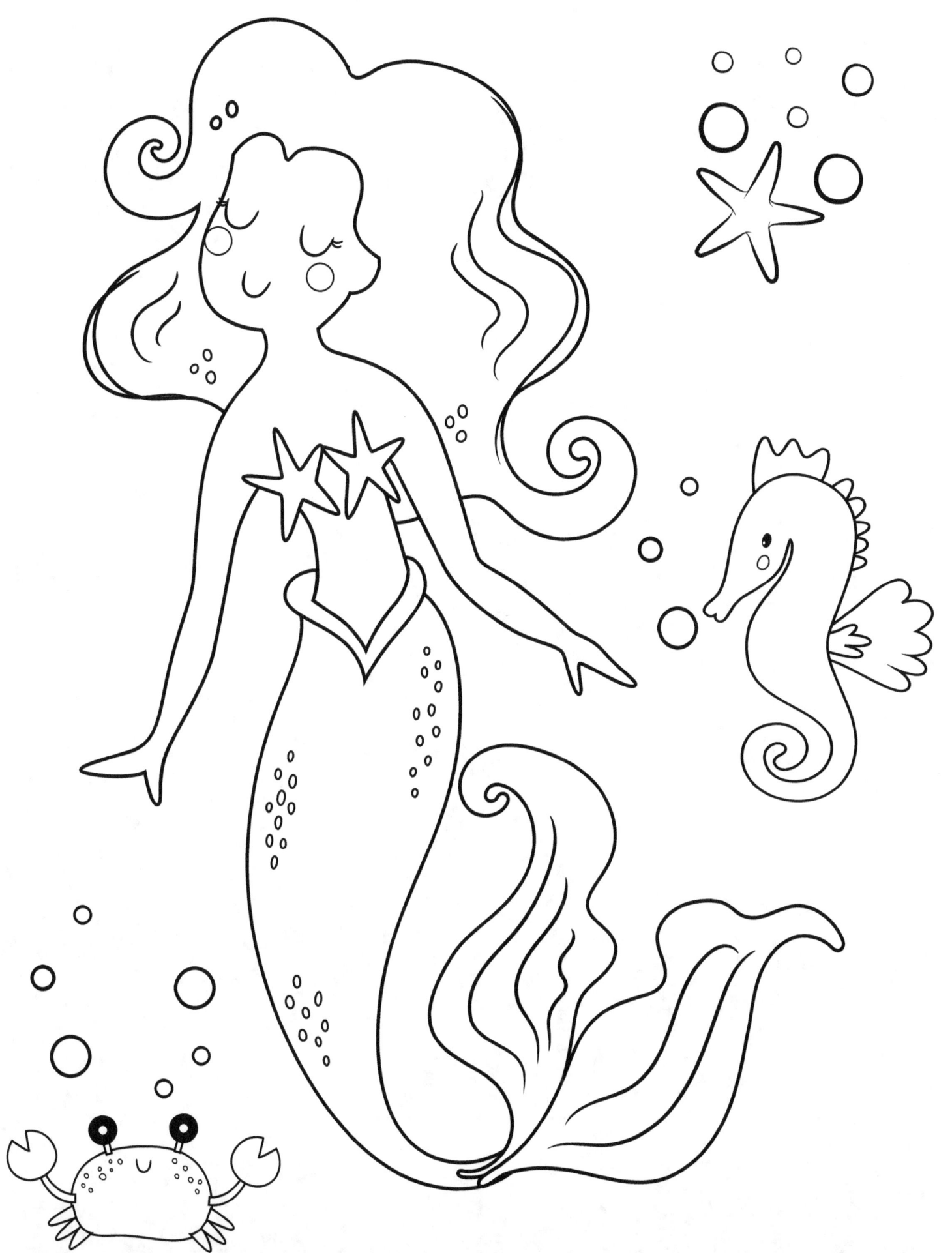

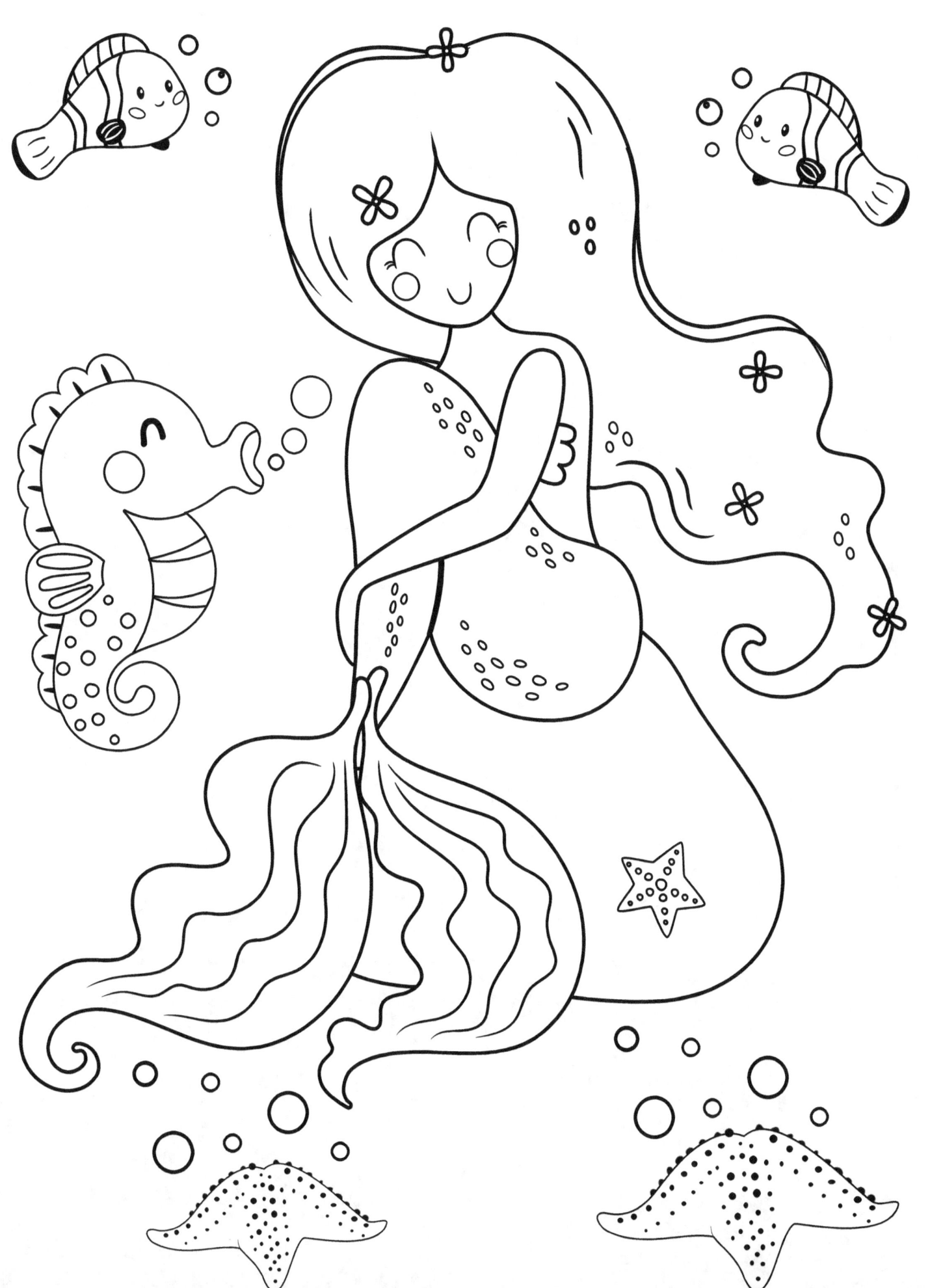

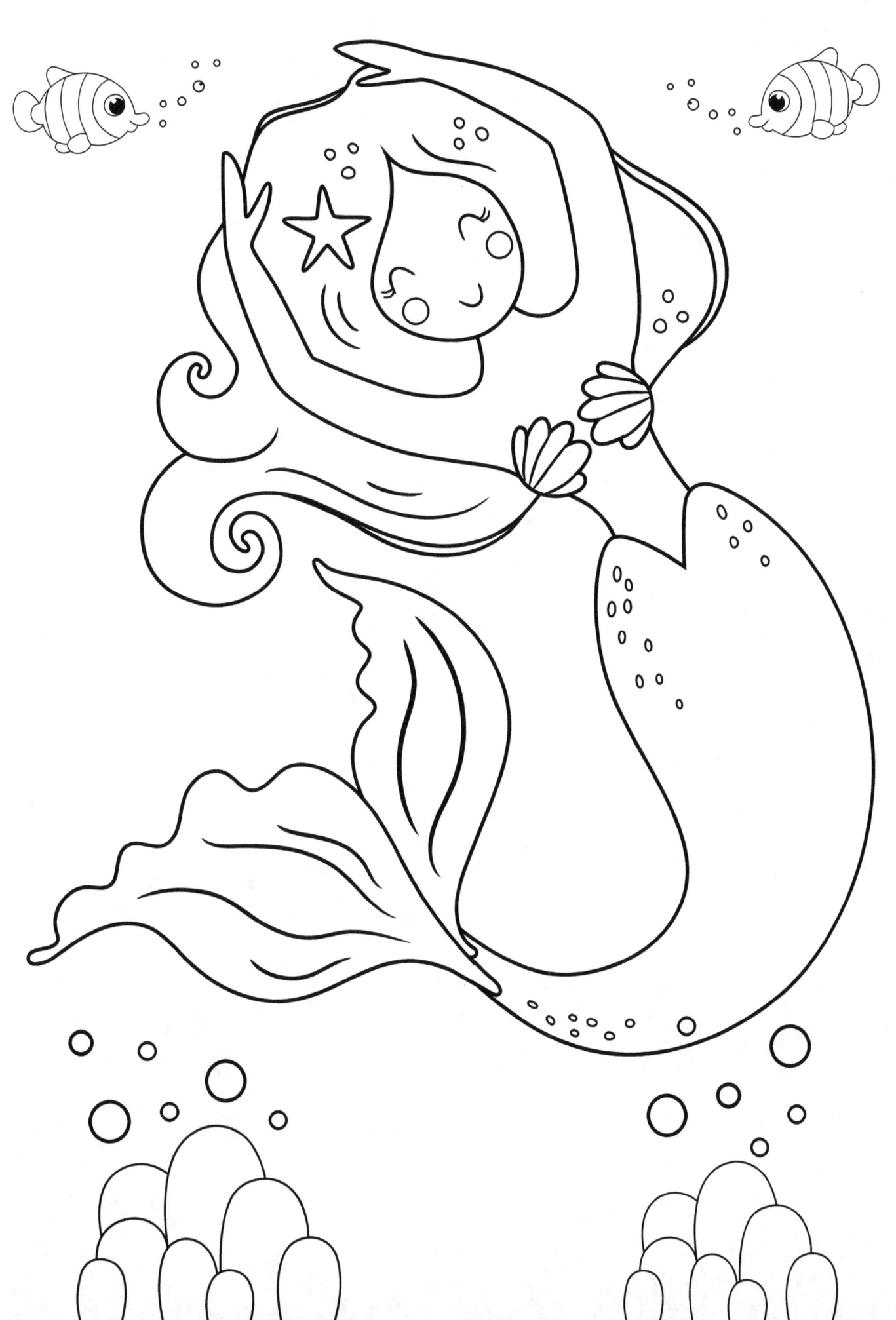

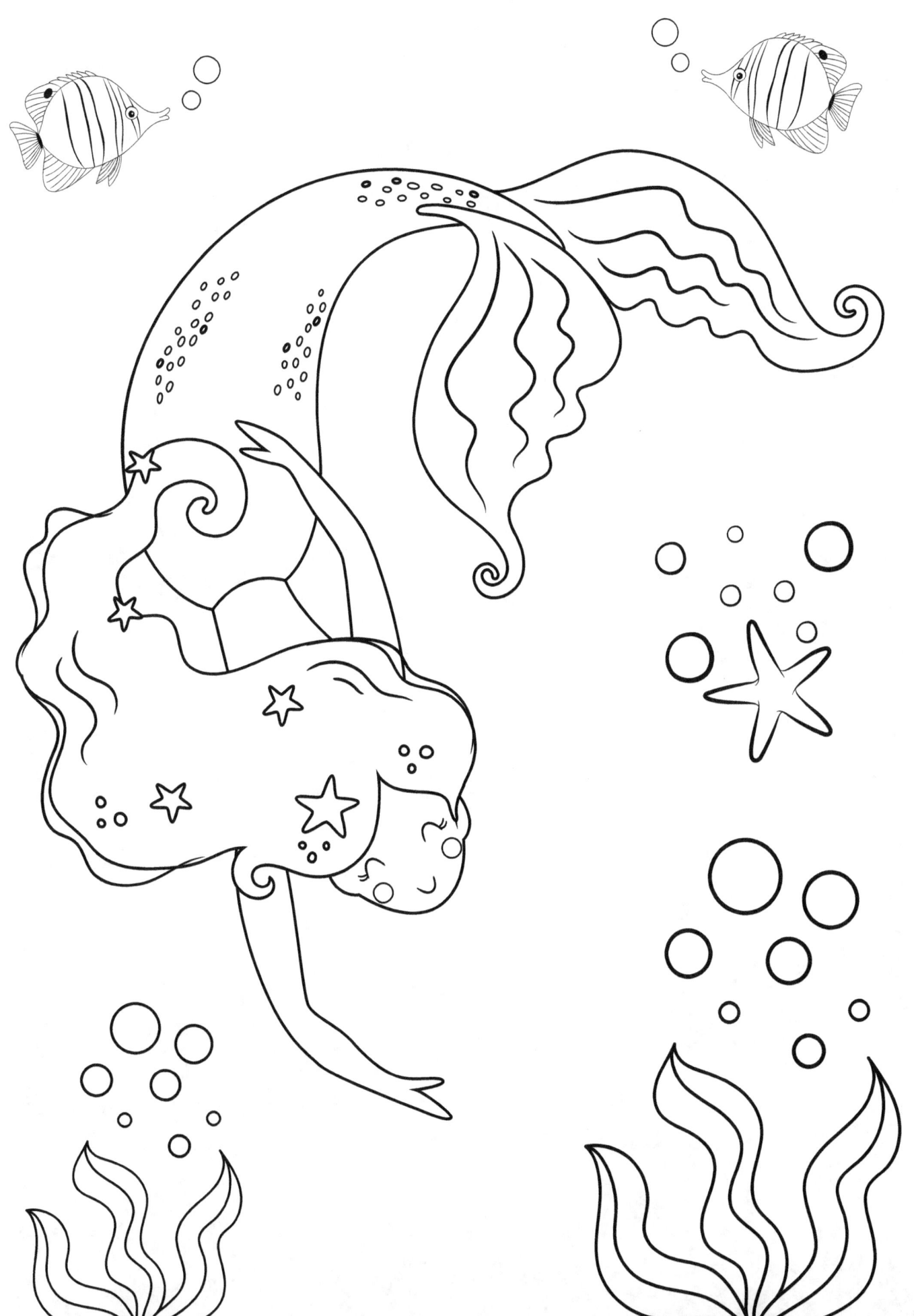

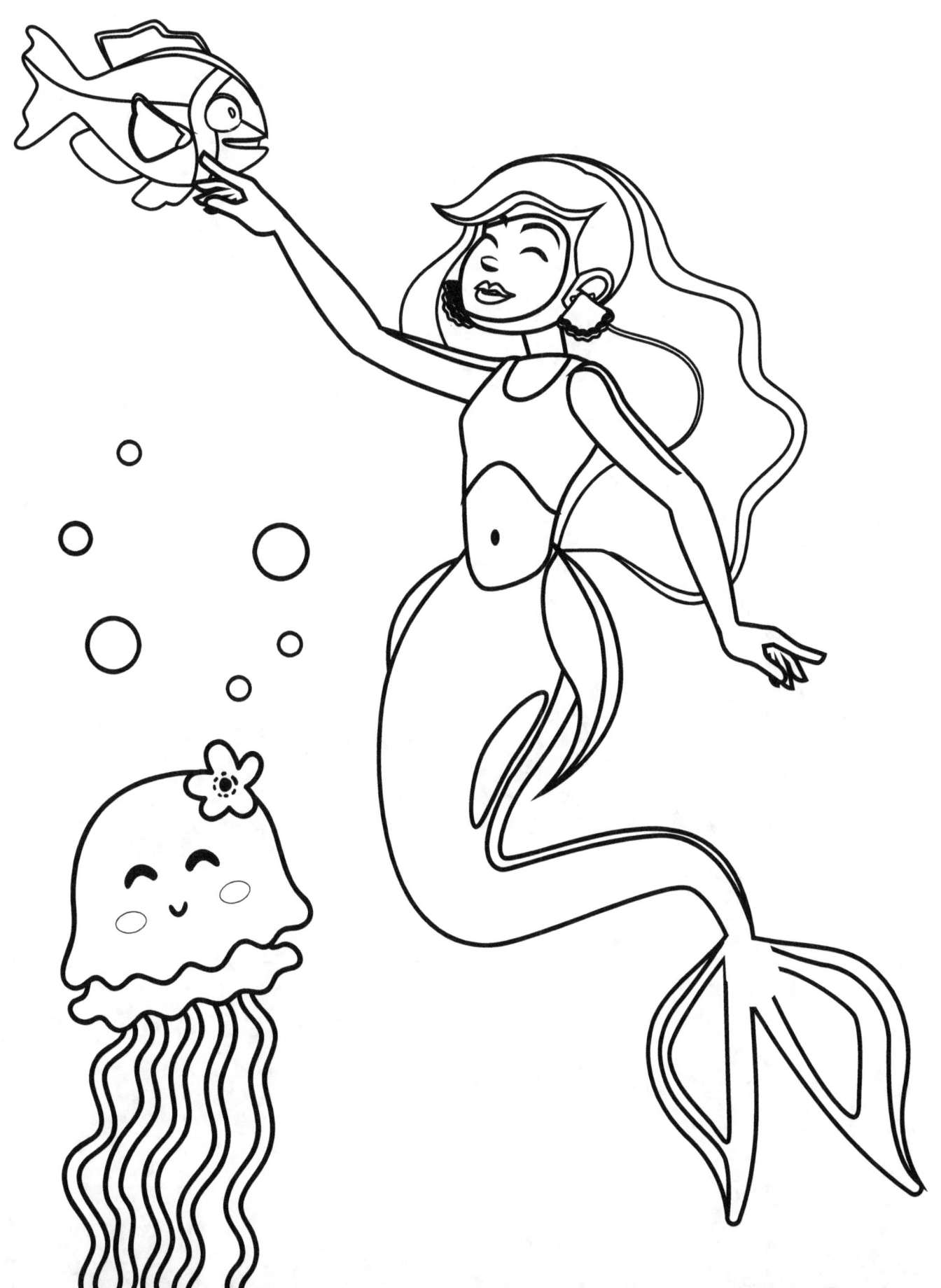

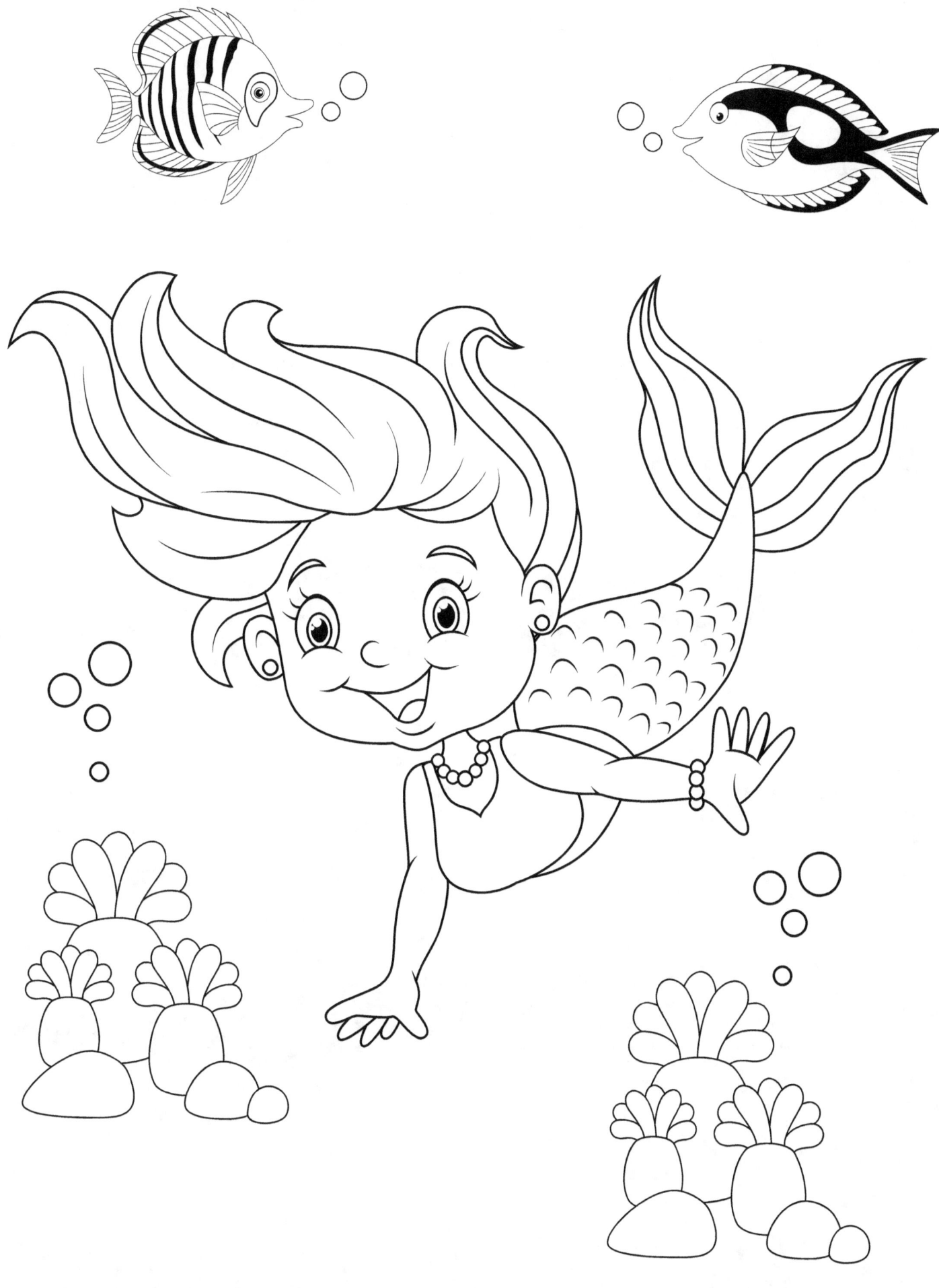

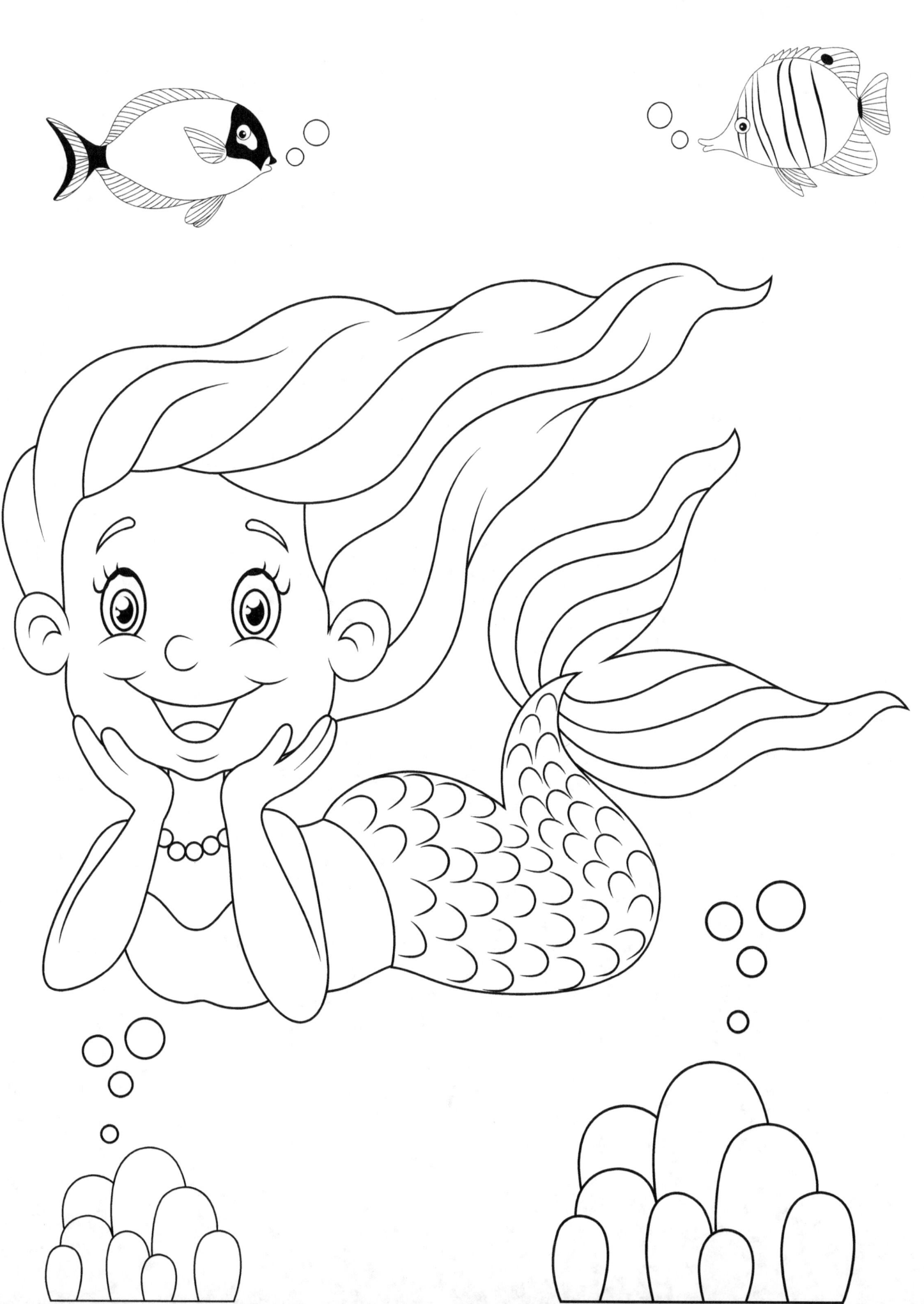

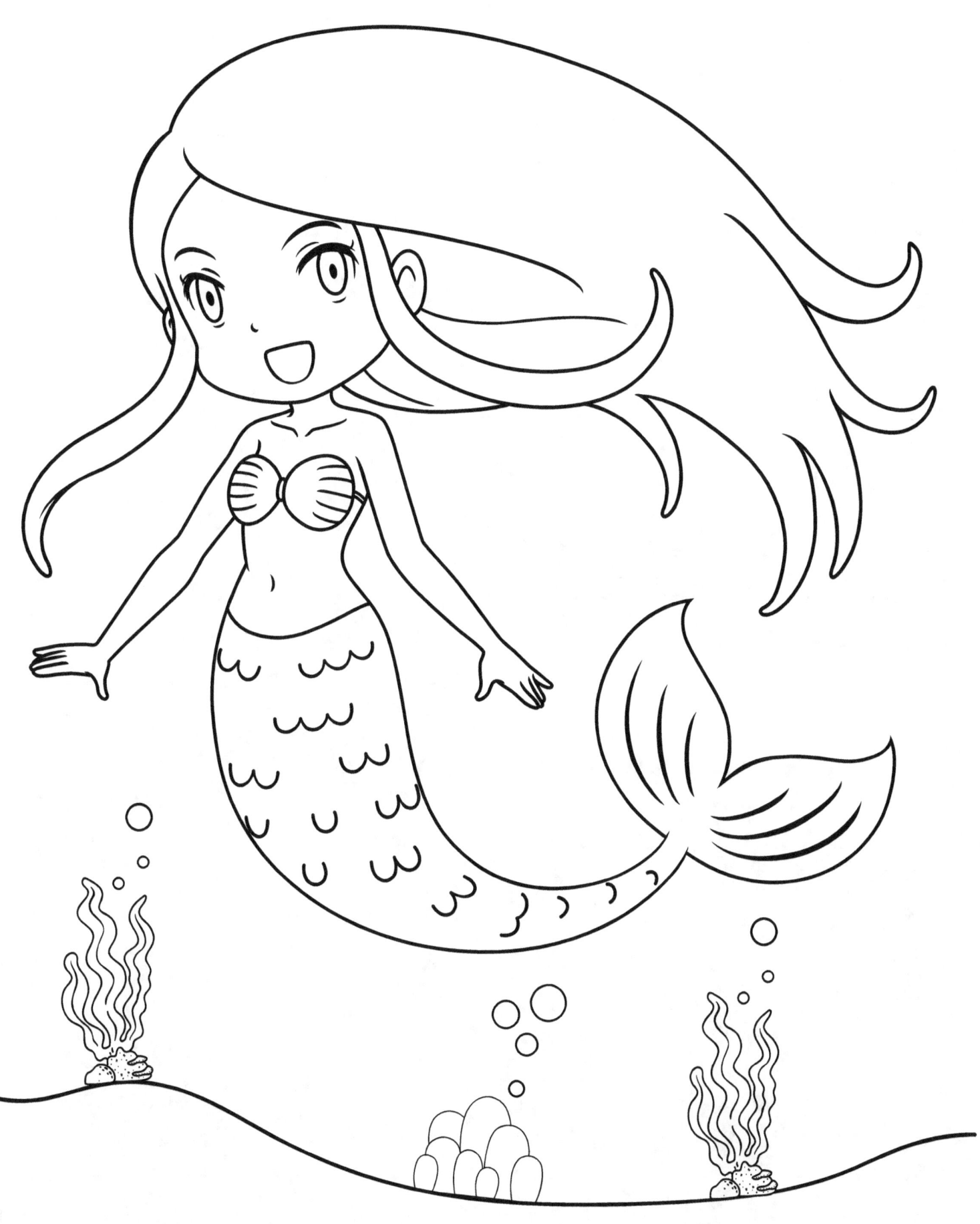

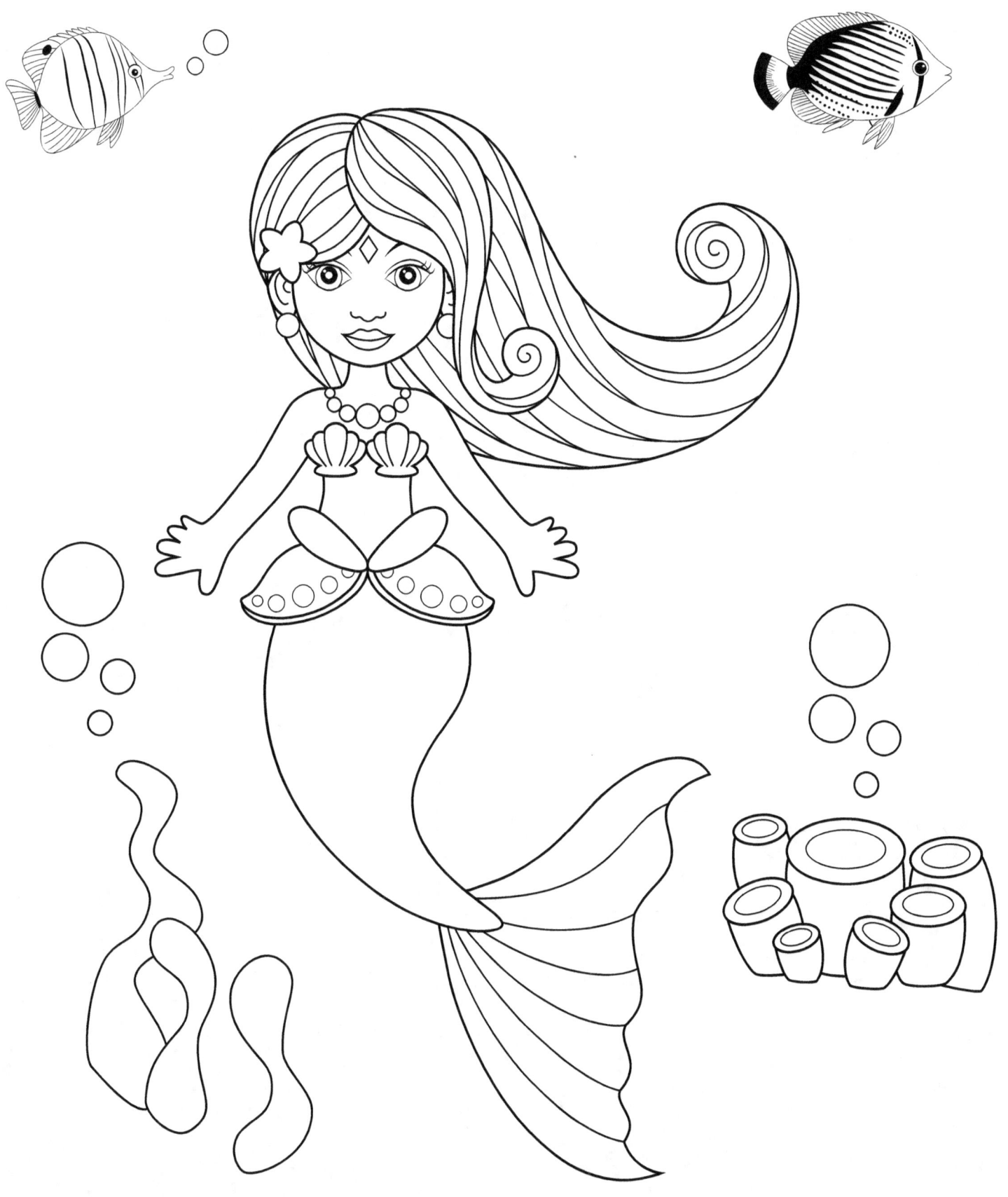

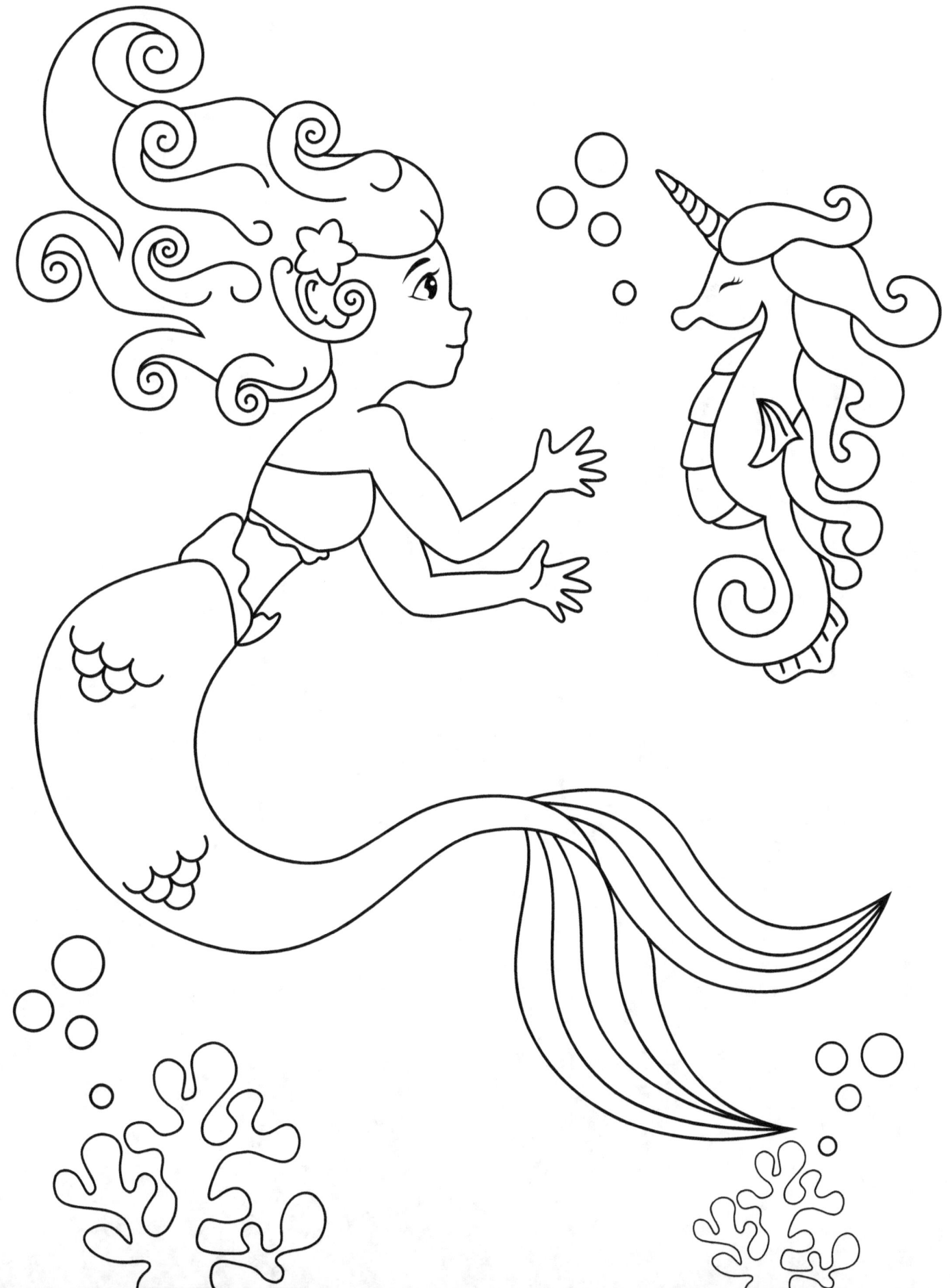

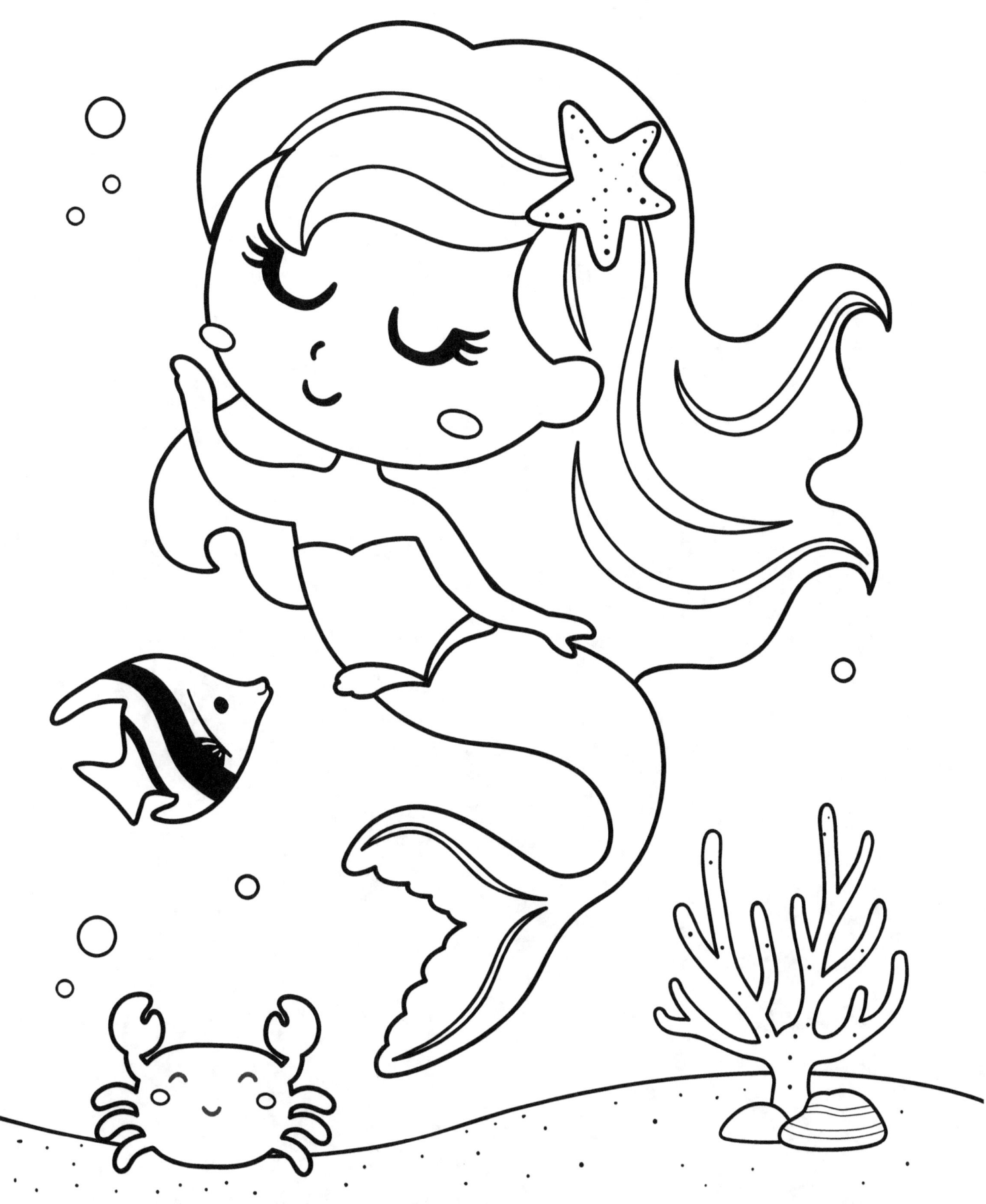

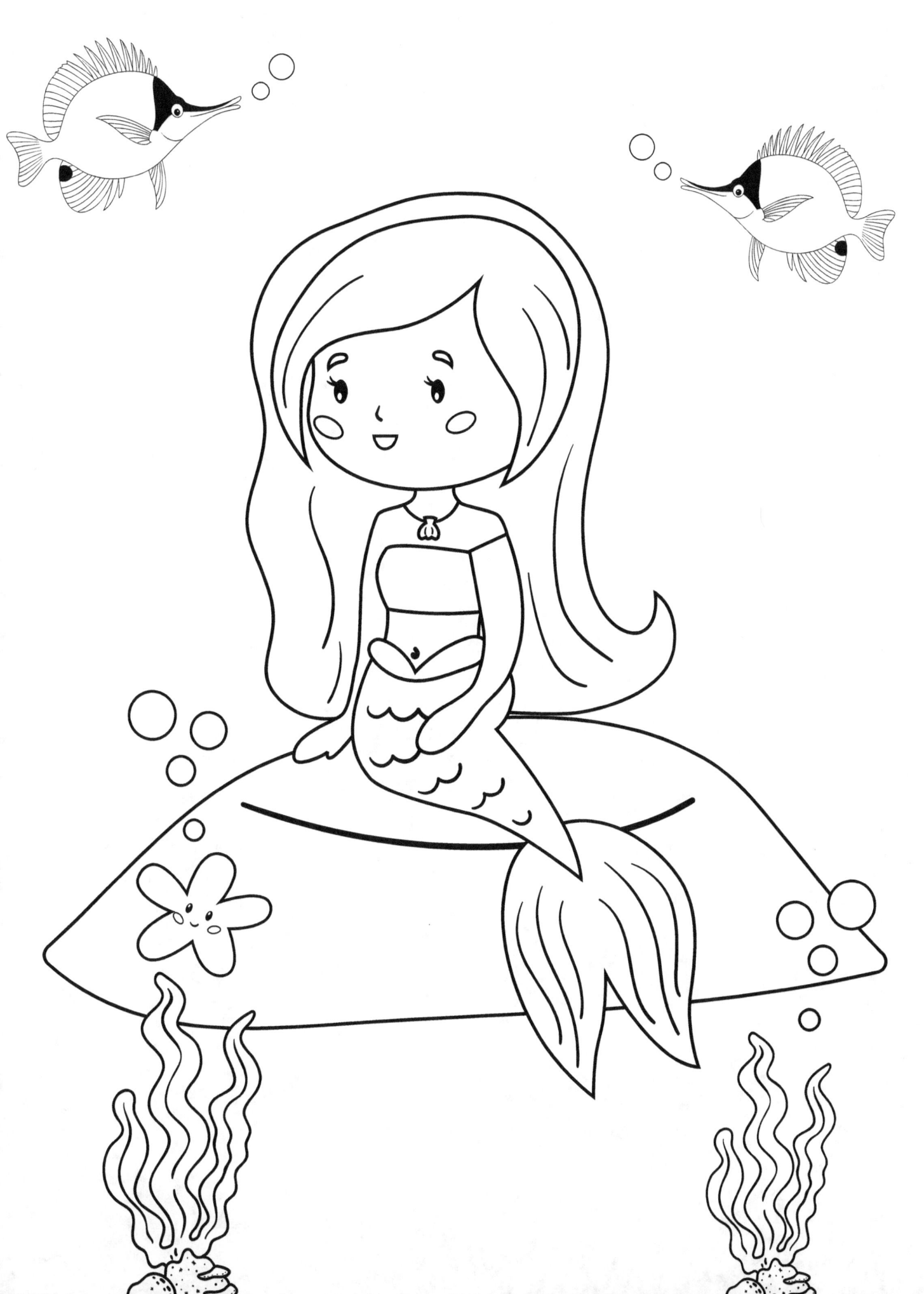

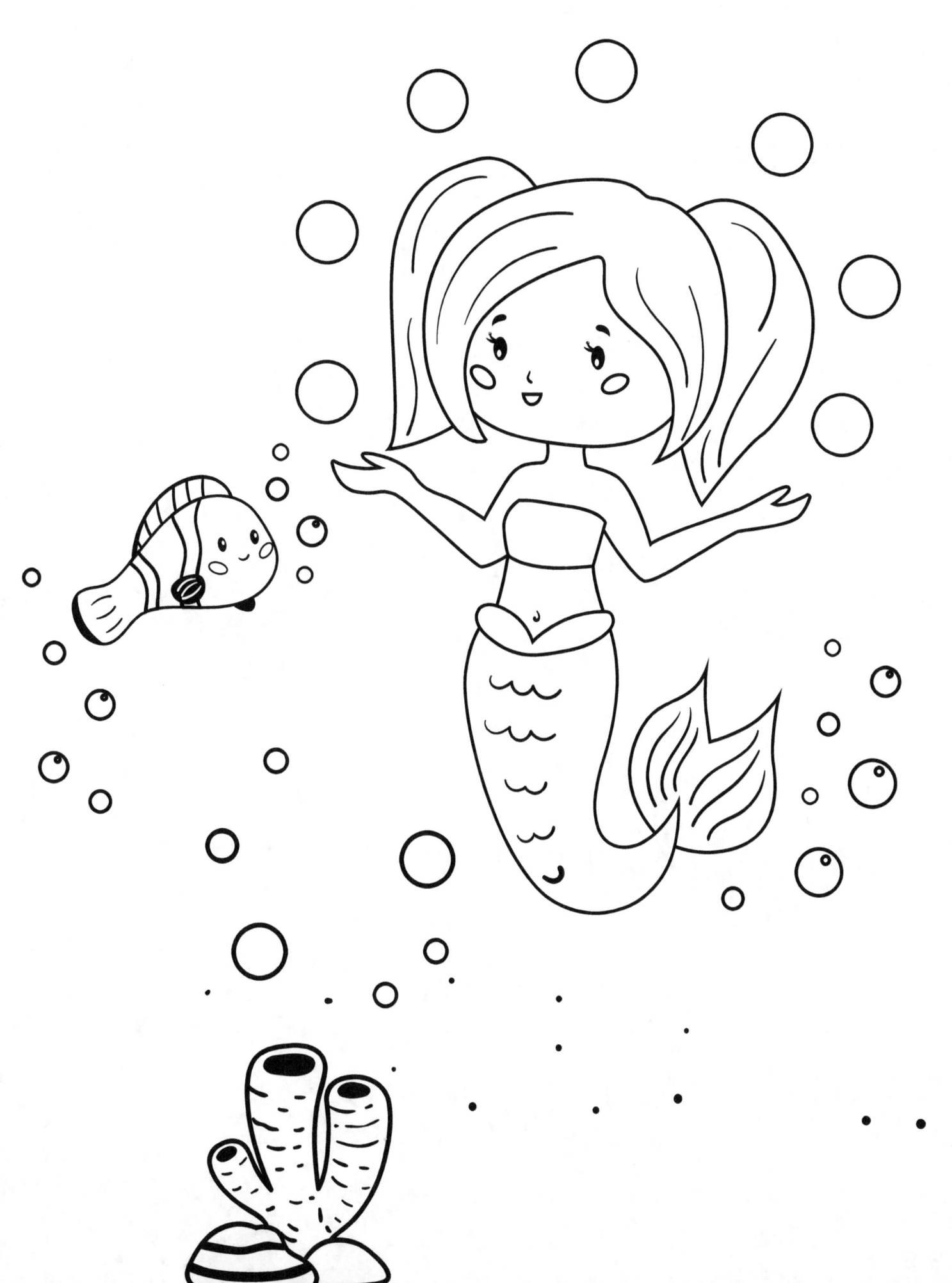

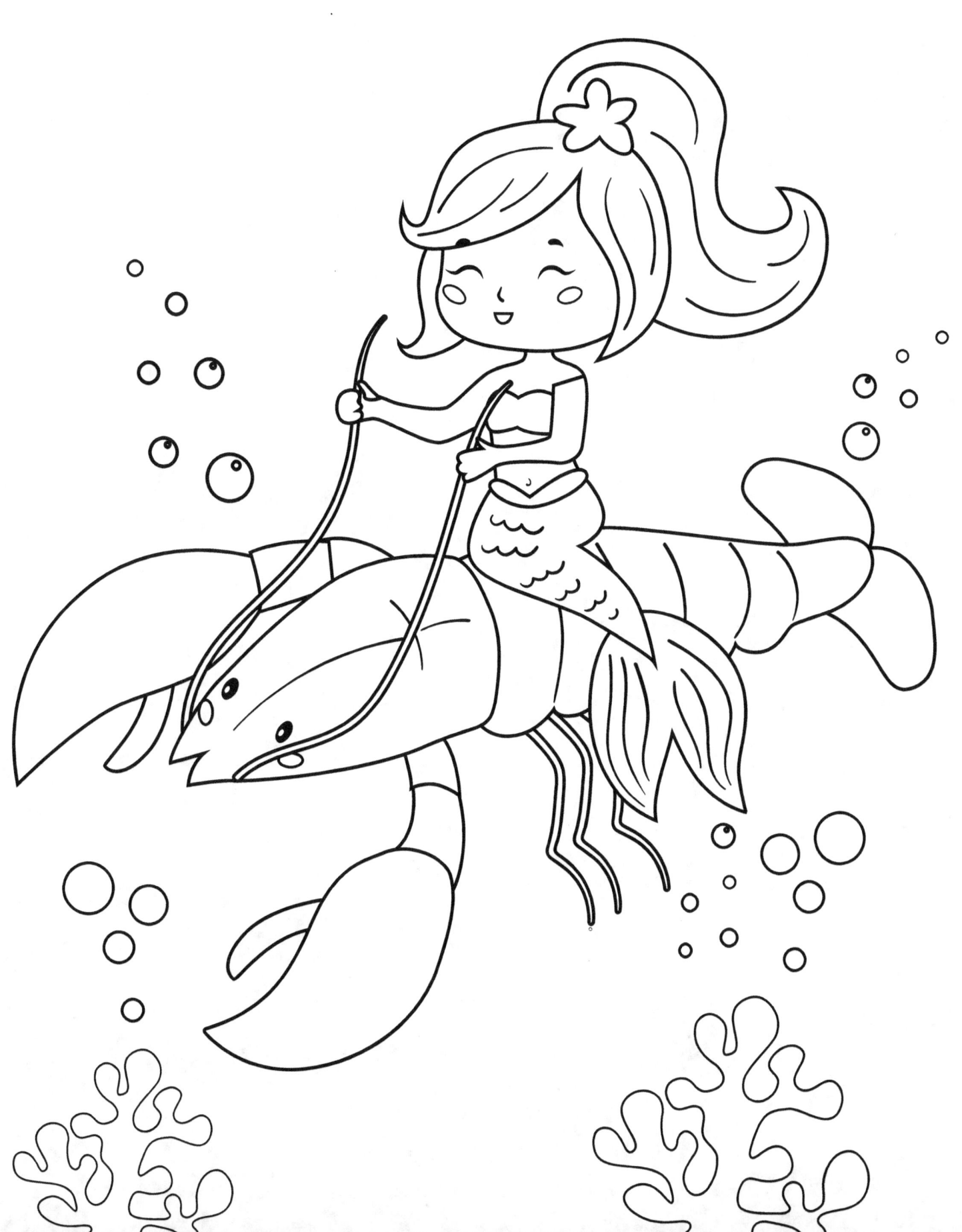

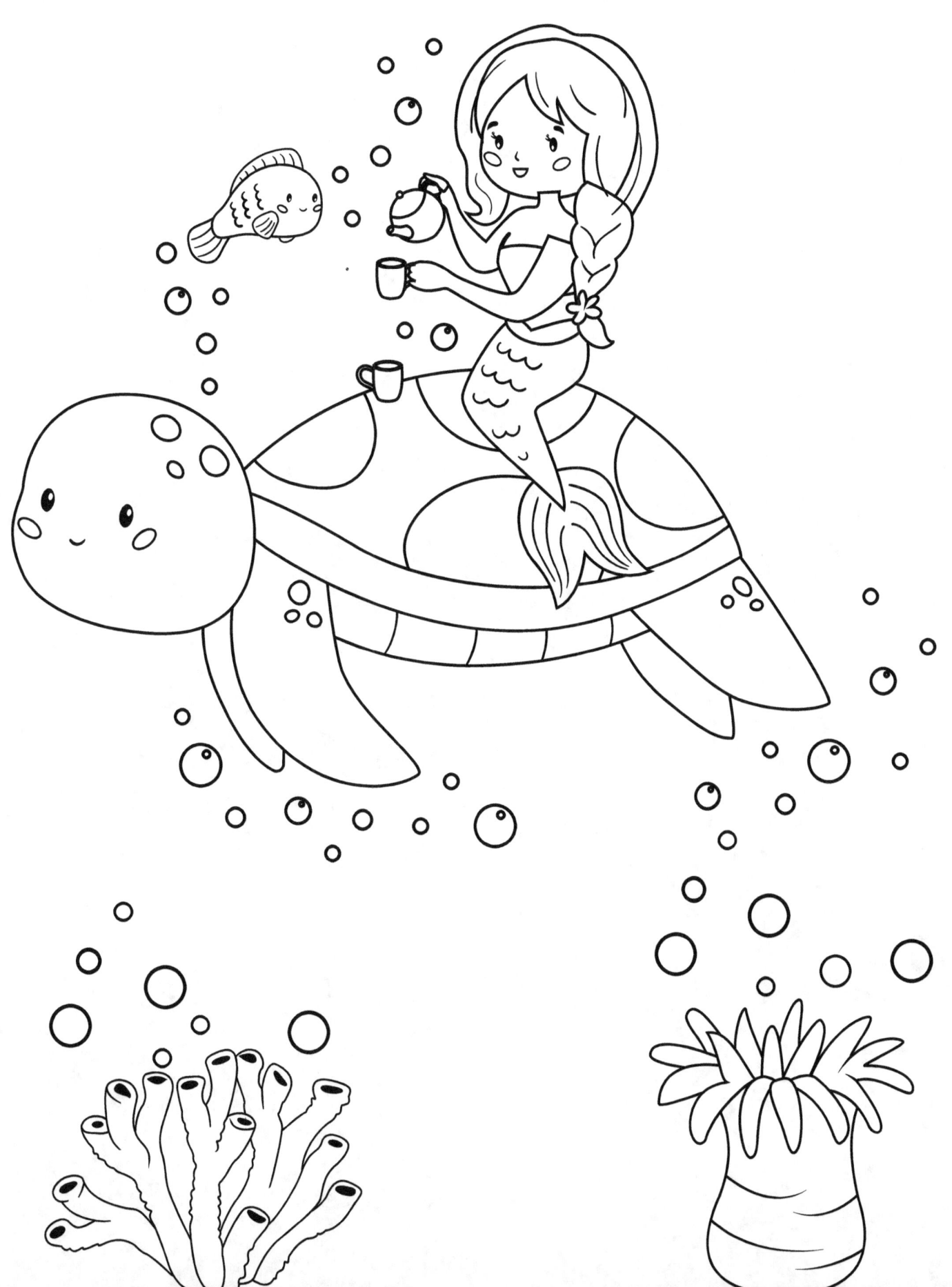

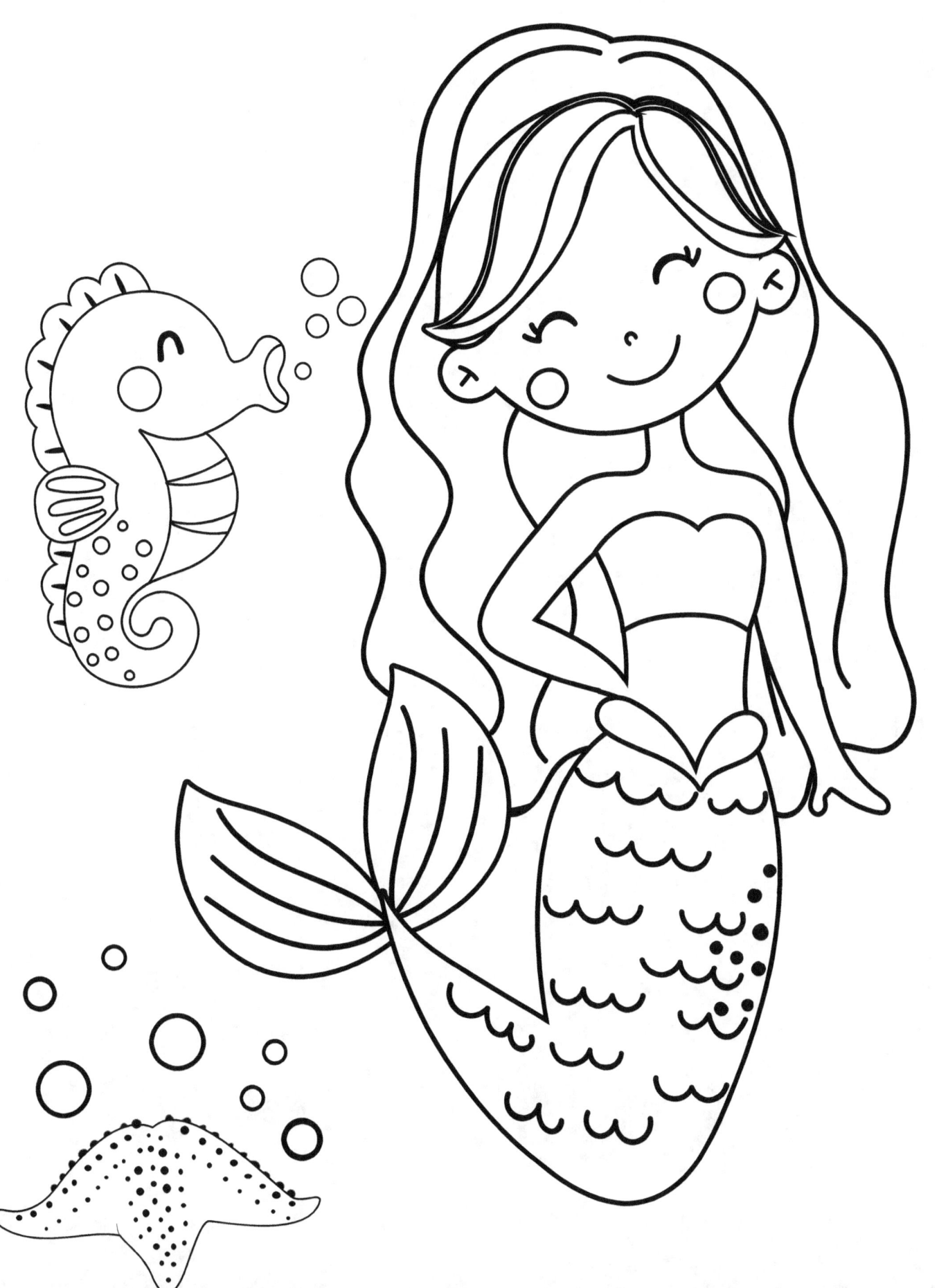

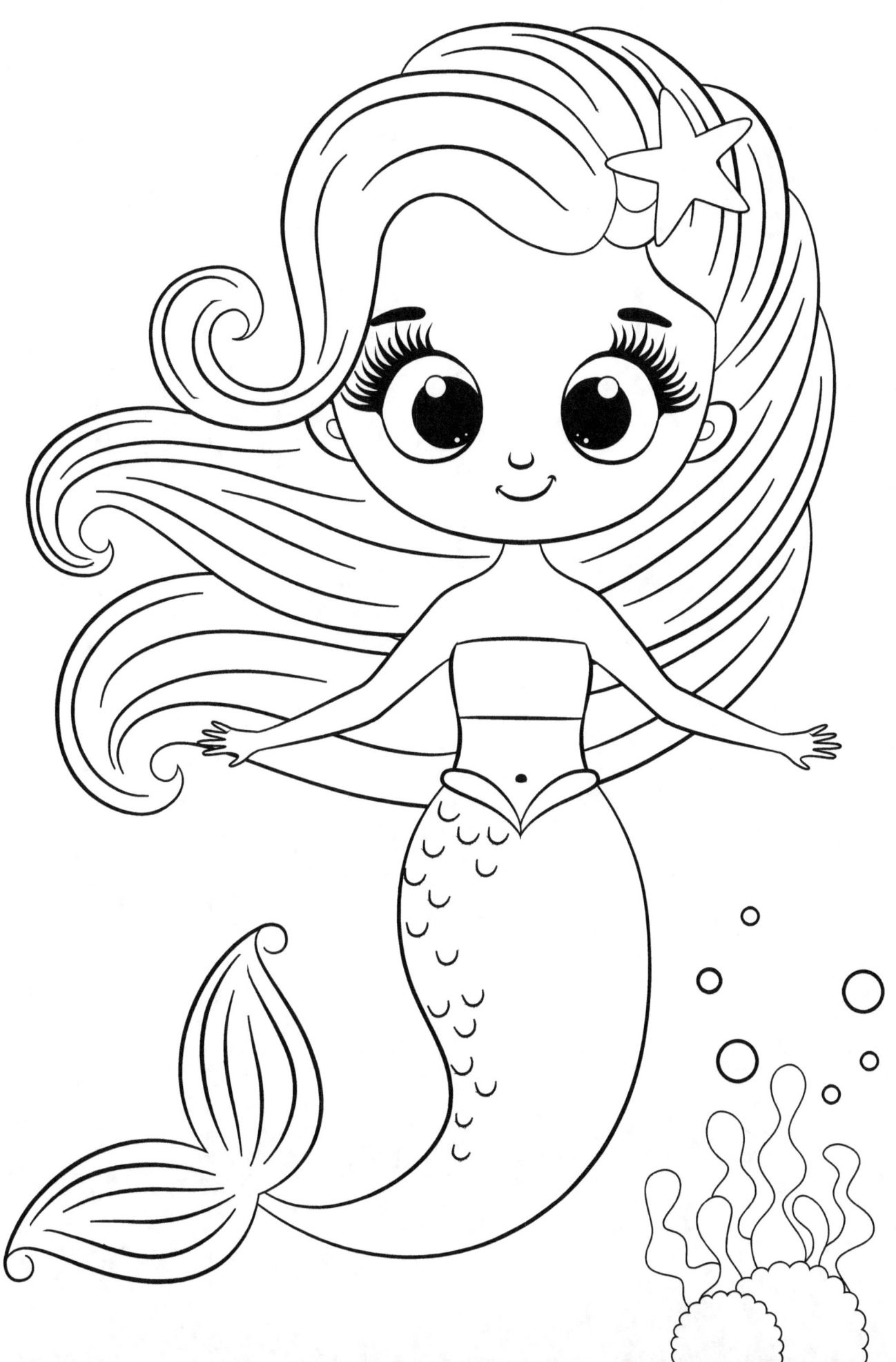

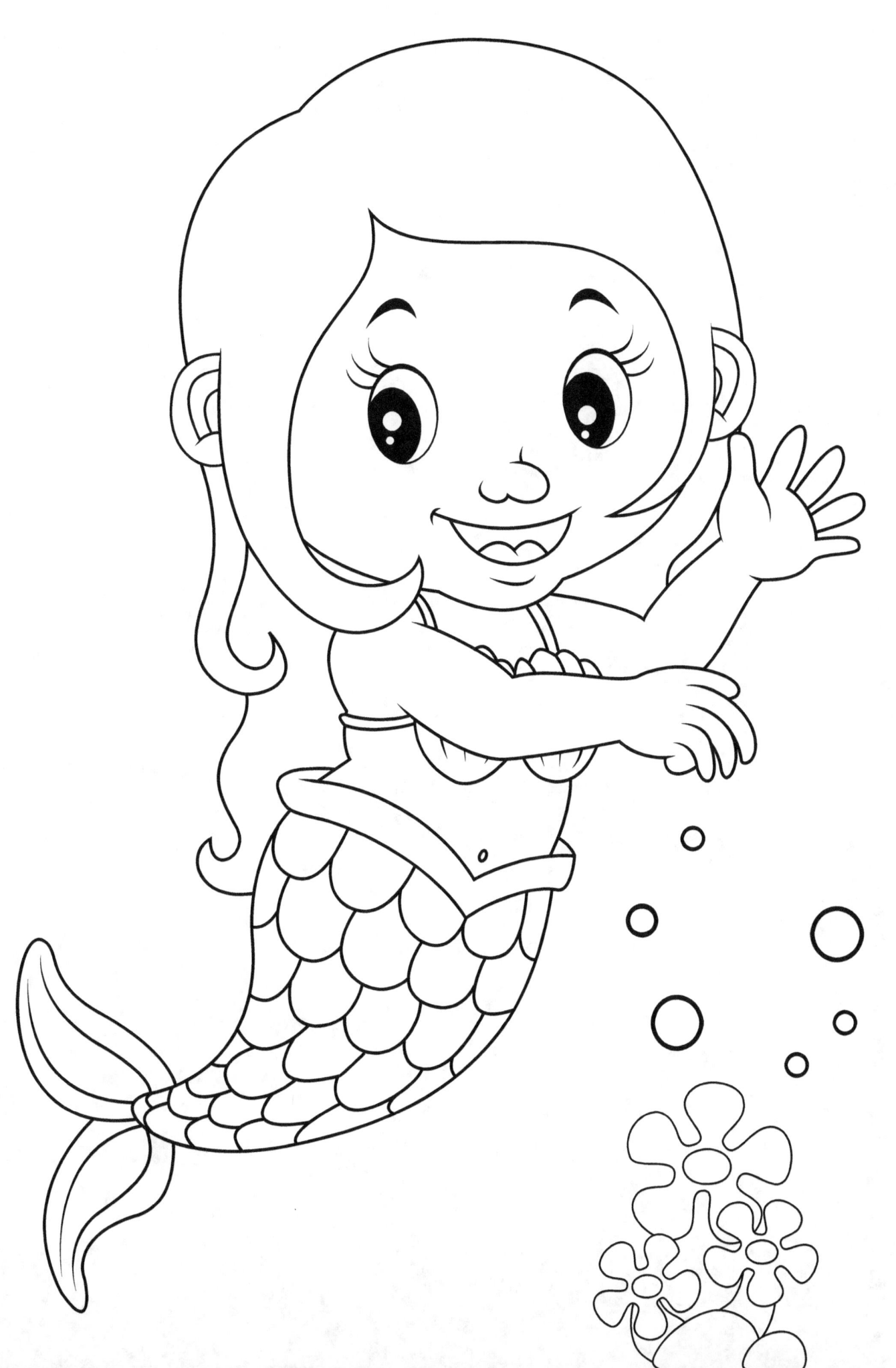

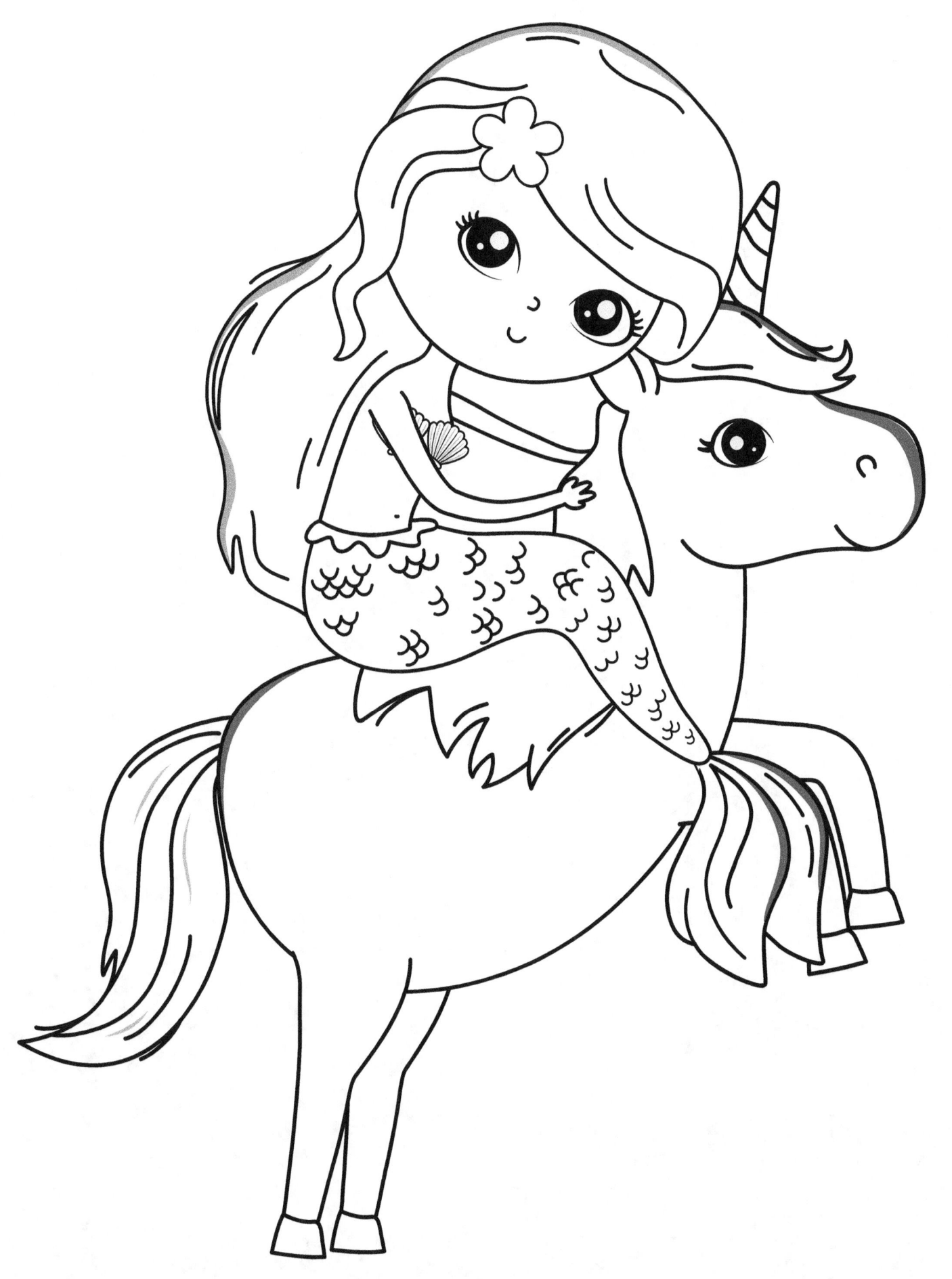